GROWING INTO YOU

A GUIDE TO LIVING AUTHENTICALLY: FIND
PURPOSE AND BELONGING BY STEPPING
AWAY FROM YOUR SHADOW AND BACK INTO
YOURSELF

Y.D. GARDENS

THE EMERALD
SOCIETY

JUST FOR YOU

~

Follow the link below to read now:
www.emeraldsocpublishing.com

DEDICATION

~

To Matt: Your authenticity has always amazed and inspired me.

Thank you for showing me that the road less travelled is also beautiful.

FOREWORD

～

As far as I can remember, I have always been curious about the wonders of the world. During my early adulthood, I became an avid traveler, backpacking through foreign countries, exploring the vast mystery beyond borders. I can recall a particular day in 2014 when I journeyed across several Central American countries. I had just stepped back into Mexico following an adventurous few days, crossing dodgy borders without much more than my Canadian passport and a backpack filled with my most essential belongings.

I stayed with a couchsurfer friend who was hosting my travel mates and me for a few nights. As we unpacked some of our belongings to settle in for some much-needed rest, I noticed that the bedroom walls were bare, except for this one wall hanging. It was a framed, thin strip of cardboard on which one could read: "*What would you attempt if you knew you could not fail?*".

This provoking statement has stuck with me to this day. I believe there comes a time in life when we must question if we are living up to our full potential. What could we change to create our best, most fulfilling life? I wondered about the extent of that statement. How often do we make ourselves the only obstacle standing in our way to happiness? How often do our thought patterns prevent us from achieving our goals? How do limiting beliefs influence our life path, how we perceive our world, and how we view ourselves?

I began to question, research, and observe others – most of all, I took a deep dive into myself. Introspection can go a long way, revealing the good, the bad, and much ugliness. As I began working on this manuscript, I realized that I was always offering to others all of which I was withholding from myself: credibility, kindness, compassion, love, and respect. I was unintentionally depriving myself of the most valuable tools to achieve a well-rounded, fulfilling life.

From the moment I fully came to this realization, I started to observe my reactions towards my environment mindfully. I was shocked at how destructive and self-deprecating my ingrained thought patterns truly were. How had I become like this? And more importantly, how was I meant to break through and move past these hindering thoughts and behaviors?

Weeks went by as I wrote and dove into research. I eventually came to realize that I was growing simultaneously with the advancement of this book. Chapter by chapter, I was rethinking what I thought I knew and applying the strategies more consciously than ever before. Writing *Growing Into You* has been a blessing in disguise. I have come to a new understanding of how crucial it is to stand proudly within yourself and expose your truth. I genuinely hope that as you flip through the pages, you will feel, as I did, increasingly empowered to move towards your goals, stand your ground, and to be authentic.

Although no large amounts of blood or sweat were shed in this book's writing, I can assure you that it has brought its lot of emotional triggers and reflections. The ups and downs of creating such a revealing and self-challenging piece of work have provided much insight into my own life. I have restrained myself from writing for many years from fear of revealing myself entirely. Ironically, while creating every chapter of this book, I have had to fight my instinctive urge to avoid exposing my truth. As it turns out, I did end up finding enough strength to power through. I fought my battle up to the very last page.

Finally, I created this first book as food for thought. It is a first step and the foundational work towards understanding how to grow into ourselves and stand strong while embracing all that we are. From psychology to spirituality, there is an abundance of aspects that influence who we are as a whole and who we choose to become. I wrote *Growing Into You* to tackle the most influential factors and provide some insight into embarking upon the next steps of your journey. The accompanying workbook, as well as the sequel *Growing Stronger*, offer more in-depth advice and tools as you progress on your path. Each of these is a valuable asset in exploring various topics as you grow and gain more understanding of the fundamental concepts related to self.

Beyond all, I wish for these words to bring you comfort in knowing that you are acknowledged and supported throughout your journey. I hope you realize that you are not alone; authenticity is a life-long voyage, and we are all in this together.

Let's stand tall. Let's stand proud. Let's stand just as we are.

～

The Calling

Long ago, when my spirit was untainted,
I danced to my own rhythm and ran at my own pace
Blindly awaiting a verdict
As to how to follow the stream,
One that would soon lead me astray from my dream

They claimed running was not for me,
My body too weak to take me where I should go.
I followed blindly, but little did I know
That my mind would soon forget how to flow.

Every step was weighed, success charted in grades;
I ran for him and for her,
I was running to my grave.

I ran to comply, I ran to achieve,

A race that was never mine;
Undeceiving, I ran as others pleased
Every single time.

Then, one day, the entire world paused,
Humanity kept to themselves for a cause,
And as patterns and long ingrained thoughts receded
I attempted to run without feeling defeated.

This time I could stop and knew I could rest;
I no longer felt being judged by a test.
Step by step, ahead and forward I went;
Unburdened, I took off without any intent.

I soared through the air, the wind in my hair.
This day was mine to seize, and old boundaries to tear.
As the rays heated my skin and warmed my soul,
I sped forward for freedom; not for a goal.

I had not stepped out in years,
How could I have been stronger?
Yet through the free flow of tears
I moved faster, and ran further.

As goose bumps rose and prickled my arms,
I knew at once they had lied;
I refused to surrender to success or charm,
This race had never been governed by pride.
It had never been about distance or pace;
The rhythm of my heart was the ultimate chase.

If I'd ignored the voices, perhaps I'd have learnt sooner
That following the crowd

Would never make me a winner.
For the battle is inside
And is our own to fight;
At our pace, it is our race -
And only we know what's right.

INTRODUCTION

∼

Through the ages, we have grown as a people because of our ability to learn from others. We are well versed at reading op-ed pieces from industry giants, reading memoirs from great leaders, and soaking up as much as we can from the opinions of intellectual titans.

As human beings, we have created complex and intricate economic and governmental systems because of our ability to study our environment, learn from it, and use this knowledge to better our lives. We have put so much into learning, knowing, and improving the world, mainly from what we learn from observing our surroundings, that it is surprising that we have not extended that same courtesy back to ourselves. Many of us have failed to learn to know ourselves. We have been unable to respect our veritable nature and to grow into it fully and authentically. How did this result come about?

Human beings run from pain for most of their lives, whether consciously or instinctively; it is in our nature to avoid suffering. We may have witnessed others make the mistake of running away from what could have been their source of liberation simply because they chose comfort and security over authenticity. They have become comfortable with a friendly version of themselves that they know, instead of facing the challenges of unearthing the version of themselves that is more fulfilled than their current state.

You see, it is normal to want to avoid pain. However, pain is vital to growth. It is merely a signal that something, somewhere, isn't right. If you experience much pain in your life on various levels, it is most likely an indicator that the life path you are following is not your main road to fulfillment. You may have been and are possibly still avoiding something. It is a signal that something has to be altered or fixed in your life before change and progress can begin to take place. Our learning and evolution can only happen when we make an effort to explore and reflect on it.

Avoiding something that is a crucial and vital aspect of your inner composition – the essence of your reason for being – may lead to many consequences. Repressing your innermost wants and needs by refusing to acknowledge them can affect you emotionally, psychologically, and physically. The whole of your being is interconnected; negligence of one aspect ultimately affects your entire entity. The beauty, however, lies in the fact that the choice to change is always yours. You can decide to keep avoiding whatever you refuse to face and continue to take the ever-increasing pain that comes as a result. However, suppose you can find the courage to change your relationship with pain and seek further, to look into the underlying issues causing this suffering and work out how you can stop it. In that case, the life-changing benefits will be immense.

Unfortunately, most of us must hit the final hurdle before

summoning the strength to face the discomfort. Avoiding suffering is such a powerful and innate component of our being. Often, it is only when we have nothing else to lose that we can face the depth of our emotional turmoil. The moment we decide that enough is enough and that we cannot take it anymore, the doorway to our salvation bursts open.

Many of us fail to realize that avoiding pain is not the same as dealing with it. This concept may seem simple enough; however, most of these mechanisms, operated by our subconscious mind, act in ways to protect us. As we instinctively use continual avoidance, our true nature becomes buried under layers of unsubstantial and superficial societal adaptive means. That little voice in our heads, our mind's narrator, seemingly becomes part of who we think we are. Ultimately, this can only lead to a situation where the pain will accumulate to a level where it becomes impossible to avoid or escape.

As many of us live under the illusion and fantasy that by running away from pain, it will magically go away, it can often come as a surprise to discover the extent of the damage we have done to ourselves. As such a low point occurs, one must realize that only one solution remains: face the music and leap headfirst into a journey of recovery. This is not an easy path, as it requires much personal investment, determination, resilience, patience, and vulnerability. It implies discovering how much harm our own ego can inflict upon our authentic nature, and how this impacts our wellbeing. However, through detachment and observation, we can take on this challenge. By doing the work and confronting ourselves, we can unravel our essence and reconnect with our innermost self.

You can have a million and one experiences, but at the end of it all, it always comes back to yourself. There is no escaping it; that dormant entity that fills and consumes your being behind all the misconceptions, traumas, failures, and losses you have faced is always within. The you that is lying motionless behind all the closed doors is waiting for salvation. You are behind the loss of your peace, meaning, and natural-born state, all of which you have forgotten. You are the only one accountable for yourself.

There is no escape outside of embracing self, and anyone who tells you otherwise is not only lying to you but also themselves. Again, avoidance cannot lead to healing. No matter how happy you think you are, you can never be truly complete until you face your truth.

The problem isn't the methods to use or the means to employ or the book to study to gain the necessary knowledge; the problem lies in whether we choose to accept the pain. The moment you consciously decide to face the hard facts and commence the journey to find yourself, you have already taken a step forward in opening yourself up to discomfort, which leads to revelations. You have now manifested that you are ready to make an effort to know who you are, even though unpleasant revelations might cover the truth. Being prepared to delve into introspection can be very painful. It may imply unleashing certain prevalent self-deceptions, such as having to own up to your life choices and accept that you are the only one responsible for your life and perceptions. It is about taking responsibility for your actions and working through the struggle of assuming the role we play in how our life unfolds.

You are always free to choose your thoughts. You can easily opt for lying to yourself about weaknesses and decide that the problem isn't with you but the world, that you're right and the others are wrong, or even that you don't need to change to achieve your goals but that the whole world needs to do better.

If you decide you are ready for change, you must be prepared to accept the pain instead of running from it, as you've done for so long. It is impossible to change something we cannot see. By exploring this discomfort, you can begin to heal and better yourself. It is only by being open about who you are, where you are, and where you want to be that you can improve.

The easy way out is choosing to remain the same person that you were yesterday. It is to convince yourself that there is no point in opting for the painful path of discovering your true self; instead, you might decide to settle for where you are right now. What is difficult and painful is to embrace the pain that comes from being vulnerable, to accept the possibility of being wrong, and to face the reality of how things are instead of living a fantasy.

The world's history is filled with stories of successful people who chose to work through psychological discomfort to better themselves and achieve their goals. They overcame obstacles and enjoyed their life with graceful ease, leaving their mark on the world because they embraced the painful unknown rather than the sweet familiar.

Why exactly do we need to know ourselves? Without knowing oneself, it is impossible to lead a complete, balanced, and fulfilling existence. The quest of a lifetime is the search for one's true self. As you simultaneously connect back to your essence and the winds of life bring about change, your feet will remain steadily grounded. Environmental and social factors will no longer shake you. You will know where you stand, firmly and proudly, confidently laying down the boundaries to your well-rounded existence. Self-awareness allows us to connect to the knowledge of specific life-enhancing attributes and capabilities. Leaving your true self buried may make you prone to incidences of mistaken ambitions, low self-esteem, poor quality of life through making choices that do not align with your innermost desires, and misplacement of priorities.

You are about to embark upon a unique journey into yourself. The time has come to turn inwards, and, if you choose to do so, to work through the hurdles. Turn inwards, deep into the essence of your being. What is so special about knowing ourselves? Are there any dangers in lacking self-knowledge? How important is it that we learn to understand who we are at the very source? What are the different avenues through which we can begin to unfold our truth and grow into ourselves? Many questions will arise on your path to self-discovery as you wonder about how to lead your journey to authentic living and towards becoming YOU. You are your solution; all answers lie within your true self.

GROWING INTO YOUR SELF

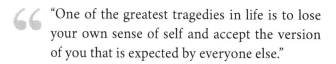

"One of the greatest tragedies in life is to lose your own sense of self and accept the version of you that is expected by everyone else."

— K.L. TOTH

SOCRATES, great philosopher of ancient Greece, once made the famous declaration: "man know thyself." This Athenian philosopher gained much wisdom and knowledge through exploring the depths of this statement. Having a sense of self is as essential today as it was in his time, if not more. It plays a crucial role in our lives. Living without a holistically connected sense of self is not living, but merely existing.

The consequences of neglecting one's intrinsically profound identity are vast. A 2017 report published by the

United States National Institute of Mental Health showed that an estimated 46.6 million (an equivalence of 18.9%) American adults battle mental illness. Even more alarming is the fact that less than half of these cases received professional help. This implies that almost 20 million residents of the United States were unable or failed to seek help to get a better grip on their life and sense of self. Anxiety disorders, impulse control disorders, mood disorders, and substance use disorders are only a few of the increasingly frequent ailments plaguing our modern society and hindering our development and wellbeing.

Psychologists have stated that a lack of sense of self is responsible for many addictive and compulsive behaviors. They posit that the early patterns of suppressing and ignoring our feelings instead of expressing, communicating, and accepting them are predominant factors and sources of compulsion and dependency.

Let's understand that these mental conditions vary in severity, and so not all of them are about significant mental issues such as depression, schizophrenia, and OCD (obsessive-compulsive disorder). However, that still does not remove from the equation that we must seek to gain a sense of self, a strong one at that, or risk falling into modern social norms, thus becoming another addition to the mental disorder statistics. It is in our power to develop a strong and infallible self-identity. Living beneath your actual value and not rising to your full potential is a tragic disservice to yourself. You do not have to live a life that is not fully and truly yours. The power to generate change is in your hands.

SENSE OF SELF

First and foremost, let's attempt to define sense of self. What is self or sense of self, and how can you build a healthy self-image? In simple terms, your sense of self is your identity: a fusion between who you think you are and what you convey to the outside world. It is your perception of yourself that leads you to make decisions and guide your life path. How you feel about yourself, your thought patterns, your level of self-esteem, and your confidence or lack thereof directly correlate to your sense of self.

Challenges are an inevitable part of life. Our sense of self or self-image plays a predominant role in establishing our response to adversity. When our sense of self is weak, and these unfavorable circumstances come knocking, we may quickly become overwhelmed by them, no matter how big or small the challenge appears. Let's look at it this way: picture a nice boat floating effortlessly at sea. The weather is beautiful, the breeze gentle, and the warm sun gently caresses your skin. Then suddenly, you notice the scenery shift: the wind becomes increasingly tortuous, the water wildly turbulent, and now the boat is being tossed about, leaving you to fend for yourself. However, you find you can breathe calmly, and you feel safe in knowing that the previously reinforced mainsail will stir you in the right direction and that the sturdy structure of your boat will keep you afloat, no matter the power of the storm.

As you've probably guessed, this boat represents our sense of self, just as the choppy waters and unpredictable winds mirror the struggles of life. Challenges are inevitable and, therefore, will always present themselves to you. However, a healthy self-image and sense of identity will provide a solid foundation for creating a life that reflects your genuine thoughts, opinions, wants, and needs. The reason you will come out unscathed and even stronger than before whenever you face challenges is that you have armed yourself with a strong sense of self. Some obstacles may leave you soaked with water or flunked around by stormy winds, but knowing the strength of your sails, you will have confidence in the depth of your power. You will have set clear boundaries and hold a firm grasp on what you are willing to let into your life. People will know who you are and where you stand.

We are nothing without identity. It is a crucial aspect of our human composition because it is what defines who we are. It outlines our life path, acknowledging where we are and dictating where we are headed. Sense of self is so wide-reaching that it will influence every area of your life. The way you perceive who you are will affect the things you believe about yourself (because yes, everything is a mere perception), the world around you, and your place in it. In simple terms, changing your mindset can alter your sense of self and essentially change your entire life.

This is why living with an underdeveloped sense of self can be very damaging. Chronic stress, anxiety, and depression are a few indicators that your self-image may need some dusting off or even a complete makeover. Signs of a low or underdeveloped sense of self may manifest through agreeing to do things you don't want to do. You might find yourself missing out on significant opportunities because of an inability to be decisive, have a constant feeling of inadequacy, engage in negative self-talk, and continually try to please everyone - to your detriment. These are all choices that sacrifice your wellbeing and ultimately lead to forging a life that is not authentically yours.

Depending on the strength of your sense of self and your perception of who you are, answers to the questions "Who are you?" or "What defines who you are?" will vary. Some might talk about their roles as mothers; others might answer by stating their area of work or professional expertise; some others might talk about their relationships and the roles they play in them, such as being a supportive friend, a present mother, or a caring daughter. Some choose to define themselves by their personality traits, such as easy-going, fun, hard-working, or intelligent. The answers we give are not entirely factual but rather a representation of who we think we are. Understand that this sense of self is something we developed very early in life. It has been tainted by experiences and trauma and, for most, solidified in emotional scar tissue as we advanced through life. Consequently, as we age and go through life-transforming incidents, they must also evolve and adjust to fit our self-concept.

WHY DEVELOP a strong sense of self?

All aspects of your life - the holistic threadwork of your existence - are laid upon the foundation of your sense of self. A strong sense of self brings about confidence and ambition and helps to distinguish you from others. As humans, we are physiologically, biologically, spiritually, mentally, and emotionally wired to strive and flourish under certain circumstances. The substructure consists of an accurately defined and well-balanced self-image and identity.

Firstly, there is a distinction between having a weak sense of self and having no sense of self at all. One is based on a faulty perception of self-worth, while the latter is often triggered by trauma occurring over periods of childhood and adolescence, resulting in a lack of or inexistence of self-identity. In either case, the impact may be a substantial lack of understanding of yourself as an individual. You may feel out of place or lost in society, perhaps empty and purposeless, weak, dependent, and lose faith in your ability to grow into a well-rounded version of yourself. In this case, it is not uncommon to continually seek outside approval and self-worth from others. The brain-fog can be so weighty and impairing that you may have no idea where your potential lies, let alone what you are capable of accomplishing.

If you do not know who you are or perhaps have an altered perception of yourself, you will struggle with managing your priorities, setting goals for your life, and being able to separate what you want from what you don't. Why? Because you have no idea who you truly are, and so cannot decide what your life should resemble. This can easily lead to a stream of misdirected life choices, which can only amount to a dissatisfying life situation. How can one possibly expect to achieve their goals and fulfill their ambitions if they don't know what they truly want?

Perhaps a need to pause, reflect, and face the hard truths of your journey this far will be beneficial. When you don't know where you are or where you came from, it is almost impossible to pinpoint where you are going.

As such, your sense of self should be continually assessed and maintained, just as you would your car, your job, your body, and your relationships. After all, it is the foundation of all aspects governing your life choices. You can do this by tuning in and listening to your thought patterns, observing your habits and behaviors, and contemplating how you respond to your environment. As you read on, you will see yourself offered more food for thought, as well as several tools to help you embark upon this process.

It is not enough to know the importance of a strong sense of self; we must also understand how to create it for ourselves. A later part of this chapter will focus on this aspect but firstly, let's discuss the factors that determine our perception of self.

FACTORS THAT INFLUENCE **your sense of self**

Humans are not meant to exist in isolation. It is within our making, as social creatures, to live in the vicinity of others and have our sense of self shaped by these encounters. This factor of societal influence plays a preponderant role in shaping our perception of self. Whatever we perceive as defining our identity is altered by psychological and societal factors. A clear understanding of these factors will help clarify how a sense of self is initially formed, how our identities are shaped, and how we can begin to make conscious decisions that lead to adjusting and molding our self-image to reflect our core values as an authentic being.

INDIVIDUATION

It was Carl Jung who coined the word individuation. The renowned psychologist defines individuation as "a slow, imperceptible process of psychic growth." Individuation is how you distinguish yourself from others. It is a type of growth that progressively brings about a more mature and developed personality. Essentially, it is the process through which a person forms a unique self, and it begins, like many things, during childhood.

Through the earlier years of our life, as we develop on various levels and interact with our environment, we can learn from our surroundings. We instinctively regulate our actions and reactions following the response from our environment. When we feel we are being heard and given room to express ourselves, we form a deep knowing that we are valuable and that our needs matter. We see ourselves as individuals who differ from others in terms of identities, behaviors, and ideas. More importantly, we are unshaken by knowing that this individuality can displease. We see our thoughts, views, and opinions as worthy of being held, within respect and understanding of the outside response. We don't doubt that our thoughts, feelings, and opinions are valid or worthy of being shared. We are well aware of and can define who we are and where we stand.

If we are not fortunate enough to grow up in a healthy environment promoting the above, our sense of individuality can turn out quite differently. An unhealthy environment that prevents us from speaking our thoughts greets our self-expression with criticism, judgment, or indifference, bringing about a weak sense of self. When our identities are not acknowledged, our feelings are ignored, our thoughts are neglected, and our ideas scorned, we may end up growing into adults who cannot see the value of their individual characteristics and beliefs.

If conditioned by an unhealthy environment to yield thoughts, needs, and wants and live according to others' standards, we may not see ourselves as complete individuals capable of communicating and affirming desires and ideas. As a result, our sense of identity can take a hit, often leading to a low sense of self.

Lacking a strong sense of self can result in depending on the feelings, opinions, and thoughts of others to lead their lives and make choices. Because they do not own up to their personal beliefs or views, they surrender (often before even trying) and become inadvertently guided by expectations and conventions. Other peoples' thoughts and opinions on what to buy, where to work, where to live, whom to choose as a spouse, and how to go about their life will continue to entrap them in a vicious cycle.

As the pattern of depending on others' opinions continues, you increasingly lose your sense of self, as you forget to reach out to yourself, first and foremost, to seek answers and guidance. This can easily lead to depression or anxiety and an overwhelming sense of hopelessness and helplessness. As individuation comes into play with building a strong sense of self, we become more aware and able to place ourselves in a position to conduct the affairs of our lives and be self-reliant. There is no doubt that happiness, freedom, and fulfillment can derive from having a strong sense of self.

ATTACHMENT

Simply put, attachment relates to how our early childhood relationships, especially with our parents, caregivers, or guardians, affect our understanding of other relationships later in life.

From very early stages, infants and toddlers will come to understand themselves within the parameters of their relationship with others. These first attachment patterns and interactions directly impact the evolving state of our emotional, cognitive, behavioral, social, and even physical health and development.

If secure and filled with unconditional love and acceptance, the attachment will bring about behavioral outcomes fashioned in a way that earns their approval. As we receive more and more affection and praise, we are conditioned to live our lives in alignment with what others expect from us and what fits their belief systems. Although mostly positive, this will unavoidably bring about a situation where we consciously or unconsciously suppress our own needs and desires and focus on granting those of our friends/family/spouse since we have been conditioned to believe that being agreeable is a way to show affection.

On the other hand, if the environment is toxic, your development can be hindered. It can leave a person thinking their entire life that their desires and needs are not valid. For example, fear of abandonment resulting from early childhood trauma can lead to an unhealthy or inexistent sense of self. It also creates insecure and emotionally reactive people who nurture a deep-seated belief that they are unlovable and inadequate. This will have a considerably negative impact on your identity development and how you handle your relationships later in life. You may find it difficult to fully accept and love yourself unless you intentionally work through the knots and free yourself from the grip of low self-worth.

The good news is that if consciously addressed and nurtured, these underlying obstacles to living with a definite sense of self can be moved to allow for healthy bonding, better relationships, as well as a more profound acceptance and understanding of others. This will bring about healthier, stronger, and more empathy-filled relationships.

Becoming a Social Chameleon

Part of the lizard family, chameleons, are famous for their ability to change colors to match their environment. With this ability, they can quickly transform to blend in, making it easier for them to evade capture and hunt their prey. Many of us employ these tactics when trying to fit into a social group or attempting to gain others' approval. Even though our veritable nature may contradict our actions and words, many of us are willing to sacrifice our core values, the essence of our being, to be part of something bigger.

Instead of having a firm hold on our sense of self, we are willing to alter our identity and beliefs to align with others. This is a trap. Eventually, a time will come when you will have been so degraded by these exchanges, by the lack of voicing opinions and making conscious choices, that recognizing or unearthing your true nature becomes very challenging.

An important factor that influences our sense of self is what we are willing to sacrifice to win social approval or conform to fit conventional norms. This factor is what I call becoming a social chameleon. In an attempt to fit into a social group, usually occurring in response to societal expectations, it is not rare for people to push their values and belief system aside. Agreeing to do things for lack of ability to say no is another symptom of this all-too-common problem. In itself, becoming a social chameleon will cause you to lose your authenticity, in a regretful betrayal of your inner truth. The need to please and the desire to fit in is a dangerous combination when it comes to factors that negatively affect our sense of self.

Self-worth and self-image are not something that we are born with; they must be carefully tended to and developed over time. For the sake of brevity, I will not embark upon the nature vs. nurture debate. However, various factors and influences, such as our environment and genetic predispositions, play a central role in determining how we develop our sense of self. We are all born with different temperamental tendencies, with which all external factors such as interactions and experiences with our environment become intertwined, forming our core self.

As we move along through life, our concept of self must continue to evolve and adapt. The more aware you become of your tendencies to blend in, thus dismissing your authenticity, the more chances you stand of avoiding falling into the trap of becoming a social chameleon.

The truth is that we can never be completely happy or fulfilled until we live our lives authentically, have the freedom to follow our hearts and embrace our instincts, and have confidence in being ourselves instead of following the crowd. Until you let go of who you believe you should be and give in to who you truly are, you will continue to struggle with your sense of self. To live a life of true freedom, happiness, and fulfillment, you have to live up to your values, care less about pleasing others, and focus on being the best version of yourself.

BUILDING a strong sense of self

Now that we've covered the significance of having a strong sense of self and the different factors that play a role in influencing our self-image, we will focus on developing a strong sense of self that aligns with our potential, peculiarities, and personality.

You see, every journey to self-awareness and self-development begins with a conscious choice to do the work and face your truths. As the proverb goes, as long as there is a will to continue, there will be a way. Below are some key tips on how to build a lasting and robust sense of self. Wherever you find yourself on this path of self-discovery, you are sure to find one or more nuggets of wisdom to add to your self-development toolbox.

DIVING INWARDS

A more significant part of understanding who you are, accepting it, and committing to improving upon it is being courageous enough to dive inwards. It is to ask yourself those unpleasant questions that you have been avoiding, face memories or facts that you have been suppressing, and seek ways to be true to yourself.

This is the point when you chose to be unapologetically honest about the discrepancy between the current state of your life and what you truly want it to be. It is a time to define your priorities, needs, and desires in all aspects of your life. It is a time to decide to grow beyond who you thought you were meant to be and who you were conditioned to become. It is the time to summon your courage and forge a vision of what feels profoundly right – and to build your path towards achieving it.

At this point, I feel it is important to mention that all things in the world outside a person are merely a projection of one's perceptions. In this sense, we create our reality. Our thoughts shape our world and our life. Your reality is a direct reflection of all that you hold inside you. Hence, the more you learn to look inward, the more opportunities you will grasp as you uncover the power that you have. You will come to the realization that turning inward is the best means of drawing close to reality, one that is of your own conscious creation.

Turning inwards helps us achieve self-realization by altering the way we view our place in the world. As you learn to find comfort within yourself, your decisional power will get stronger, and you will come to embrace obstacles and fully own the directional control you hold on your life. As you settle into your authentic being, you will come to a place of understanding that your life does not have to be ruled by any external factors. This is excellent news. Diving inwards will make you the boss of yourself! No longer will anyone else be accountable for your successes, nor your mistakes. It is a package deal and one that comes with great rewards. You will see that you are so much more than what society has shaped you to be. There is so much inside you that you have yet to tap into.

Right on the inside is where truth resides as against all the noise, confusion, and lies that exist on the outside. Finding yourself is taking a front seat to your thoughts and witnessing all that has been holding you back. In all aspects of your life, the awareness behind the confusion will be revealed. Building self-image comes from looking inward; it is the only place where your true self can be found.

THE POWER of Affirmations

As you navigate towards gaining and strengthening a sense of self, knowing and having confidence in who you are, learning how and when to say "no," and learning to focus on caring for yourself, you will discover an array of tools at your disposition to support you along the process. I have come to use two highly useful and impactful tools daily: positive thinking and affirmations.

Every day, negative thoughts run through our heads. There is no avoiding this fact. However, depending on how we approach these thoughts, they might take up residence in our head or float on through. Allowing them to stay and dwelling on and nurturing them - can be very damaging to our psyche. Some valuable tools that can help us redirect or transform these unpleasant thoughts into neutral or positive ones are mindfulness, gratitude, visualization, and affirmation.

Positive affirmation, visualization, and gratitude have a way of altering our thought patterns. This process is very powerful and can even result in a complete alteration of our physiological responses. As we live in a fast-paced world that has us continuously stimulated by a flow of irrelevant stimulation, most of us come to deal with stress and feelings of anxiousness as a regular and permanent part of our life. Unless you live a highly-secluded lifestyle with little or no responsibilities, stress is an omnipresent aspect of everyday happenings. It is essential to understand the mind/psyche is intrinsically connected to the physical body, and changing one will impact the other, whether negatively or positively.

Positive thinking and mindfulness are conscious approaches to altering your thoughts. Yet, this can become an automated response with regular practice and eventually carve a path to the subconscious mind.

Daily affirmations help boost your confidence and make you feel like you can accomplish anything you set your mind to. There are plenty of recipes already created in this area, but you can easily make up some of your own as needed.

Affirmations are positive personal statements that promote self-empowerment and vary according to your individual needs. They should ultimately lead to a situation or goal that you would like to turn into reality. By repeatedly saying or visualizing these statements, we can change our perception of our environment and alter our mindset. It then becomes natural to detect the circumstances that will lead to your vision, and therefore instinctively seize an abundance of opportunities. You will soon find that your ideas have become your reality through a simple shift in mindset; a whole new world has now opened up to you.

There are some straightforward tips to help include visualization into your daily routine. Whatever your need, you will find there is an infinite number of affirmations at your disposal. For the purpose of our journey to self-discovery, the following propositions will help ground and center yourself and foster a balanced perspective of who you are. As most of us begin and end our day in bed, it is easy to include these statements at those precise moments. Here are a few examples of clear and concise and powerful statements:

- *I am ready for transformation.*
- *I welcome this emerging entity that is my essence.*
- *I am taking responsibility for my life.*
- *My sense of self is growing.*
- *I am open to a shift in energy in my life.*
- *I am grateful for the opportunities and life lessons that come my way.*
- *I invite authentic connections and abundance.*

As you will find in the accompanying workbook, there are numerous options readily available. However, the most powerful ones will undoubtedly come from yourself, as you picture your desired goals, habits, circumstances, and so trigger their realization.

I strongly advise that you carefully select statements that you can easily visualize. Affirmations and visualization go hand in hand and are powerful tools in discovering and embracing your true self.

Creating a Vision Board

Once you come to understand who you are and where you stand, you will be able to clearly define where you want to be. Your next step is to give wings to your plans. It is time to take action and challenge yourself to reach your goals. This is where a vision board comes into use. If you have begun to work with affirmations and visualization, this will come naturally into play. As a concrete tool to envision your life (present, short-term future, and long-term future), your vision board will mainly comprise details of the daily activities you must carry out to realize your goals.

So, what are vision boards? Simply put, they are a concrete visualization tool for realizing dreams, desires, and goals. This process usually involves finding or creating pictures and images representing your aspirations and collating information on a board. Doing this will enhance the visualization process, thus creating a more positive outlook on your life's potential. It will make you prone to attracting more of what you desire into your life by altering your mindset and propelling you to get to work to turn these dreams into reality.

Vision boards are inspirational and incredibly powerful in bringing to reality that which we desire and setting forth tangible ideas, dreams, and goals that you hold of yourself. Your vision board should be easily accessible and within sight during most of your day. This will allow your brain to fully process these goals and transfer them to your subconscious mind, where they will seed and flourish. Before you know it, you will realize how much your life has shifted without much of a conscious effort to do so.

SELF IN SOCIETY

We live in the age of social media, TV, and high-level fashion, where we are constantly bombarded with images of what, who, and how we should be. Our environment is so polluted with negative and superficial information that even those with strong self-esteem can easily fall prey to these capitalist temptations, leading to a spurious life of people-pleasing instead of staying true to ourselves.

A strong and firmly rooted sense of self is key to leading a balanced life and highly beneficial to personal growth. It will allow us to go through life without being pulled right and left by the many external influences that seek to make us other than who we truly are. Armed with a solid sense of self, we can face adversity and come out stronger; we are able to live a life of value and self-fulfillment, achieving our goals and continue moving forward.

2

OWNING YOUR TRUTH

"You either walk inside your story and own it, or you stand outside your story and hustle for your worthiness."

— Brené Brown

It is in our nature to crave respect, dignity, and acceptance. In trying to achieve these things, we put ourselves in positions where what matters to us becomes secondary to what matters to others. Ignoring our feelings and emotions while seeking to gratify those of others becomes second nature.

We often mask how we feel inside because we're afraid of what others may say about it, or because we are fearful of being the recipient of their judgment, rejection, or unfair opinions, we hide away our feelings and desires and steer away from vulnerability.

What if we could live a life of authenticity, integrity, and honesty? What if we could live a life that is true to our values, principles, and inner wisdom instead of one based on others' opinions, expectations, or views? Now, understand that owning your truth isn't about "fixing" yourself. No one is broken; living life in itself is a work in progress. Our journey is unique and of substantial value. So, owning your truth is not about finding fault in who you are or the choices you have made. It is about stepping fully into the here and now. It's about owning the moment and choosing your own direction, almost as if you were the only existing being on Earth. Time to unshackle yourself from the prison of self-doubt and inadequacy. It's time to find your way to becoming the powerful, confident, and unique person that you are.

How can you become confident in yourself and not shy away from your truth? I will admit that it is a daunting process, one that will require you to step out of your comfort zone continually. Just as overcoming any fear, owning who you are to the fullest necessitates acknowledging that you have not been living authentically. Oh, the lies we tell ourselves! It is fascinating how we manipulate our thoughts to avoid tricky situations or make ourselves feel better. Single. Day.

But is it possible to remove the gap that exists between who you project to the world and who you truly are? Well, as is said, there is no more sure way to fail than never to try. Let's dive into the concept of owning your truth, and you may just find what you seek.

EMOTIONAL INTELLIGENCE

One essential ingredient for living a life of success, happiness, purpose, and fulfillment is emotional intelligence.

Some psychologists will argue that one's emotional quotient can be more impactful in determining success in life than the intelligence quotient. Some of the components of emotional intelligence are self-discipline, self-regulation, social skills, motivation, empathy, and this other factor that just happens to be our main area of interest: self-awareness.

There is no doubt about it: every individual is different, to some variable extent. We have different personalities and possess different needs, wants, and desires, with endless ways of expressing them. To successfully navigate these various aspects and correctly express them takes a certain level of cleverness and tact, one that does not necessarily fit the mold of intellectualism; in fact, it may well escape the understanding of those who experience life with a firm hold on rationalism. That is the wonder of emotional intelligence.

These different aspects of our lives are affected by certain factors, and so are expressed differently depending on what these factors are and how we respond to them. When you are emotionally intelligent, you know what you are feeling, understand what these feelings are telling you, see how these feelings affect others, and figure out how to express them correctly. Emotional intelligence is far beyond understanding your own emotions; it also involves perceiving and appropriately translating those of others.

As mentioned earlier, emotional intelligence is shaped by critical areas of personal and interpersonal skills or competence. Self-awareness is one of these factors and may even be described as the foundation on which all others are built.

SELF-AWARENESS

What is self-awareness? According to Daniel Goleman, self-awareness refers to the ability to understand your own emotions and their effects on how you interact with your environment. A self-aware person is not only capable of understanding their emotional responses as they happen but are primarily (and more difficultly) able to witness them from an outside observer's viewpoint. This is a powerful and challenging feat, as we are innately programmed to respond to and from emotions. Watching and monitoring how they evolve becomes a key to self-regulation, which helps maintain a focused and clear mind, untainted by extrinsic triggers and perceptions. You will see your emotions as an automated reaction and thus have a stronger hold on the extent of the emotional response to any given situation.

Apart from being aware of and making sense of your emotions, self-awareness also allows you to express more empathy as your understanding of your environment grows. Grounding into yourself, you will not feel the need to raise defensive shields and protect yourself from your environment. Sure, it will leave you susceptible to pain and quite vulnerable, but as you will soon discover, this is a crucial state of reaping the benefits of growing into yourself.

EMOTIONAL SELF-REGULATION

Mindful recognition of your reactions and emotional patterns is an essential step in the right direction, but it is a whole other challenge to express them adequately. This is where self-regulation, which we can also call self-management, comes in. As we move forward in this process and develop a better understanding of our emotional responses, self-regulation, a process by which you manage and adjust to environmental stimuli, naturally pieces itself into the puzzle. This creates a direct connection to learning how to manage or regulate your emotions properly.

Overreacting is an example of failure to self-regulate. Reframing negative thoughts is vital to having a clear outlook on your outside world, leading the way back into your true self. Life experiences can be confronting and testing. However, it is always within your ability, first and foremost, to modify your response to any given situation by conscious choice. I find it fascinating how much of our power evades us. As most of us grow up in a society defined by strict expectations, rules, and guidelines, we often forget the extent of our innate abilities and come to reduce our decisive power in making our life our own. This can lead to emotions being expressed in an unhealthy way, or at least one that does not serve us.

IMPROVING your self-regulation skills and living your life with dignity go hand in hand. This means that as you embark on this journey towards growing into your authentic self, you will work simultaneously on your ability to identify and mindfully manage stress triggers and find tools to center and ground yourself.

BEYOND ALL, let's not forget to nurture our feelings and emotional responses, as they are essential responses to lead us into wellbeing. Through daily habit management and observing our thought patterns, we can tame these instinctive and wild emotional reactions, living our lives one step ahead of them. I assure you that this is massive progress towards living authentically, as you will no longer be a victim of your brain's chemical reactions to stress. Adversity and challenges can become your allies when you understand the angle from which to greet them.

. . .

DISCARDING victimization

Studies have shown that one of the most significant factors affecting mental health is what psychologists call "internal locus of control," mainly taking responsibility for anything and everything that happens to you. It is a belief that you have control over what happens in your life and that you are not a slave or a victim of outside influence or power.

A healthy sense of control is a product of being able to firmly say "no" without feeling sad or guilty, exercising the right to set your own priorities, protecting yourself from harm, getting what you pay for (we don't always get what we think we deserve, and such is life), choosing healthy relationships, and creating your happiness in life. Not happy with something? Change it. Once you stop making excuses and come to take full responsibility for your circumstances, you will gain a sense of executive power and feel more centered.

EMPATHY

If you must genuinely own your truth, it is not enough to understand your own emotions or how best to express them; you also need to learn to understand others' feelings and be prepared to adapt to them. It is important to respect other people's right to own their truth and sentiment that comes from a place of empathy. Empathy is the capacity to see things from others' perspectives; to put yourself in their shoes.

Unfortunately, as a general rule that I was reminded of throughout my childhood, one cannot give what one does not have. This means that if you do not feel love towards yourself, it is highly improbable that you will be caring and openly loving towards others. Now, you are not condemned to carry this burden for all of your lifetime. As soon as you begin to alter how you perceive yourself and allow yourself to be perfectly flawed - a masterpiece of work-in-progress, I like to say – you will notice how finding beauty in everyone, and everything becomes so much easier.

Everyone is entitled to their own opinions and ideas. I am not saying you must accept certain behaviors, nor does it mean you should validate, condone, or sympathize with what others say and think. Remember, ideas are mere perceptions of a shared reality. Imagine observing cloud formations on a summer's day; one person may spot a dragon-like cluster, while the other can only find a flower-shaped cloud. Perhaps a third person sees nothing at all. This shows how one person's truth does not validate, nor does it invalidate another's.

Another thought on empathy: it is not always necessary to feel pain to understand it. Sure, you will be better equipped to relate to someone's feelings if you have been through a similar situation. But then again, we do not all react the same way to one given set of circumstances. So many factors come into play; it would be pretentious to assume that everyone feels and responds equally. One remarkably common misconception is how we assume that everyone thinks the way we do. But we'll dive further into that later.

Finally, empathy is a significantly important interpersonal skill that helps us interact and connect with others. With this skill, we can communicate better and build stronger, healthier, and more meaningful relationships. It is beneficial for those around you and incredibly helpful in your path to self-love.

. . .

Knowing your truth: **personal value systems**

As a focal point of this journey, knowing your truth makes an appearance on many levels of self-development. This is because failure to define the parameters of your life can have dangerous consequences. It can lead to a complete loss of your sense of self, impacting life-goals and ambition, relationships, mental health, and overall wellbeing. To embrace a life that is truly yours involves going through a process. I cannot hide that your findings may be confronting, and your truth may first exasperate you before it sets you free.

Finding your truth implies knowing who you are, what you want, and what you stand for. It entails understanding the actions and behaviors you must put forward to become whole. Standing firmly behind your values means not feeling the need to justify your actions and decisions. It means being unapologetically you.

By now, you understand how focusing on what other people expect of us and repressing who we are only to accommodate others' needs can lead to the loss of sense of self. Consistently repressing emotions, impulses, wants, and needs that reveal our true self has devastating effects on so many levels. The truth is, knowing who you are involves accepting how you feel and connecting with your deepest values. Betraying your values is equivalent to betraying your-self. Defining a clear set of personal values or a value system is a central component of the foundation upon which you grow as a person. It will affect all aspects of your life and clarify what you expect of others and, most importantly, yourself - in any given situation. There is no other way around it.

If you truly want a fulfilling life, you have to start by understanding who you are. As you pause to reflect on your path so far, you may want to put pen to paper (or keyboard to screen, whatever floats your boat) and ponder what truly matters to you. What are you willing to accept in different areas of your life, and where will you draw the line? This means tackling career, relationships, physical and mental health, and all other vital aspects of your existence. It means knowing what your nature and core essence are, what makes you tick, and what gives you a sense of fulfillment and self-worth. Nothing can be of more service to yourself than knowing where you stand and who you are.

SPEAKING **your truth**

Oh, the challenge. When did it become so difficult, so daunting, to come out and act like yourself? How did it become such a challenge to be proudly opinionated and debate one's point of view, passionately and respectfully? Knowing your truth is one thing, voicing it is another. When you chose to live authentically, your actions and words are naturally in alignment. This is a direct consequence of your clearly defined value system and promotes a healthy and well-rounded lifestyle.

Speaking your truth applies to all areas of your life. There is a certain level of power and freedom that comes with being able to speak your truth. It's not necessarily about challenging people or getting in their faces (even though I will admit that it sometimes may be quite tempting) but rather about self-affirmation. The time has come to lay down the law, and you have my utmost blessing to do so within your value system. Set down your boundaries, and abide by your decision to embrace who you are and what you believe to be right. You may not always be right; in fact, mistakes are a welcome personal growth factor. Oh well, you live and learn. Be kind to others, and before all, be kind to yourself. We are all a work in progress.

Opinions always have and always will differ. There is nothing wrong with a healthy expression of one's thoughts, within the knowledge that they are perceptions, not facts. Let's move to a space of compassion, where we allow ourselves to evolve at our own rhythm as we dance to our own beat.

Our truth runs deeper than any opinion, for it is about how we feel and all that matters a great deal to us. Speaking your truth isn't about being right; it is about expressing your mind in a transparent, authentic, and vulnerable manner and allowing yourself to be heard. It is about self-respect.

BEING UNAPOLOGETICALLY authentic

We live in a society where we are always expected to follow the crowd, adhere to popular opinions, seek to please others, and value others' views. Would it be wrong to believe that these expectations can hinder our wellbeing? It may be how we've been programmed to act, but certainly not how we were meant to live. The truth is that we are free to be our own person, free to love ourselves for who we are, and free to be unapologetically authentic. As we are not programmed to think this way, it is a process of self-development to undertake. Just like speaking your truth, being unapologetically authentic is a choice to express yourself as a whole and unique individual.

The most genuine ways to experience living authentically are numerous. Refusing to apologize for having opinions and for experiencing emotions is a great place to start. There is also much to be said about belittling yourself, which has unfortunately become a synonym for humility. It is an absolute shame to witness people full of untapped potential knock themselves down to avoid impeding others' egos. This is often done to gain acceptance and to avoid confrontation and is an absolute barrier to self-development. If you can find the strength to be unapologetic, authentic, and whole-hearted in the way you go about your life, you are more likely to experience fulfillment and happiness.

According to Brené Brown, an absolute legend in this field, being authentic is about making our own choices; the choice of being honest, and the choice to let the world see our true selves. Until you have learned to value yourself, you cannot ask others to respect and appreciate you. Let me emphasize that this does not necessarily mean putting others before yourself. It is a balanced approach to a healthy life-style. Until you pinpoint the things that are holding you back and make an effort to clear them out, you cannot truly be yourself. Until you you're bold enough to refuse to give in to the self-limiting factors of self-doubt, shame, and fear, you will never live to the level of your true potential. The deci-sion is yours to make.

Understand that you have every right to refuse to be held down by popular opinions and societal expectations. You are allowed to reject the social paradigm which dictates when and how to appeal to others. Instead, choose to focus on what you want. Be concerned about being happy and fulfilled, and have no doubt that this will spread, for joy is highly contagious. Focus on things that put a smile on your face, and bring peace to your being. You are allowed to do away with anything that forces you to hide behind anyone's shadow or to make yourself less than you are.

Live fully. Be free, grasp every magical moment, and land into yourself. Let your authenticity be known. I encourage you to build your inner-strength and to solidify that unshakeable confidence that inhabits you. Connect to the most real and most profound part of who you are so that you can better understand what you came to this life to do. When you can make this deep connection and embrace the resultant discovery, you will no longer be bound by the need to be accepted by others. When you achieve this, nothing can stop you.

Our journeys are unique. No one else will get to experience what it's like to be you. You are in the most privileged position; embrace your power, and find peace in knowing that you were always intended to be none other than yourself.

Having the courage to be vulnerable

Imagine, for a moment, that the law firm where you work has just given you the nod to represent your first client in court. You did your very best to prepare for the case, but when the first court day comes, you see the legal team's quality representing the other party. You suddenly become nervous and fidgety, hands trembling, heart rate increasing, palms sweating. You become overwhelmed with certainty that your hard work won't pay off, that you will look foolish, and that you will struggle with making your case.

This experience highlights a situation of vulnerability, one that is not uncommon in our fast-paced, productivity-centered existences. These situations lead our body and mind to respond by resisting confrontation or avoiding the challenge because, let's be honest: no one enjoys public humiliation. Often consumed by our ego, we succumb to the temptation that is avoidance. However, avoiding confrontation, avoiding vulnerability does not build resilience. It does not make us stronger and certainly does not favor our path to self-reliance and acceptance. All those progress-hindering thoughts such as You'd *better turn around and go back home*; *You are not ready for this*; *If you speak, you will make a fool of yourself*; *what if you fail and people mock you*, come from a place of vulnerability. By pushing yourself to go through with the process, even with the possibility of being judged, mocked, or ridiculed, you are allowing yourself to experience something not only transformative but also healthy. In the words of Brené Brown, "vulnerability is the core, the heart, the center of meaningful human experiences."

After spending many years studying vulnerability, Dr. Brown came to this beautiful conclusion: "What scares us is sometimes actually good for us, and if we can stomach sitting with it, vulnerability has the potential to transform itself into joy." Vulnerability is what we experience when we are bold enough to step out of our comfort zone. It is a feeling that permeates our being when we attempt something that challenges us. It is the ability and willingness to entertain the emotional uncertainty of being right or wrong.

While putting ourselves in situations of vulnerability may be seen as a sign of weakness, that is not actually the case. The truth is that it takes an infinite amount of courage to accept to be vulnerable, whether it is exposing our truth within personal relationships, admitting when we are in the wrong and asking for forgiveness, opening up to others, or taking on new career challenges. As an automatic protection mechanism, we all possess a strong urge to avoid situations that make us emotionally exposed and vulnerable. Nevertheless, we must understand that this vulnerability is the foundation for creating many of our heart's desires, including self-fulfillment. It is when we put ourselves in a position of vulnerability that we can fully (and authentically) experience joy, courage, love, creativity, a sense of belonging, and empathy.

While stepping out into that courtroom to represent your client may make you very uncomfortable, it offers you a golden opportunity to expand and lean into your discomfort. It holds the potential to lead you into discovering new things about yourself, to grow personally and professionally, and develop new habits. A valiant First Lady once said: "No one can make you feel inferior without your consent." The power to take what you will from any situation is within your hands. Embracing a space of vulnerability can be life-altering and incredibly empowering.

YOU ARE ENOUGH. Let me repeat: You. Are. Enough. So, put yourself out there. Let yourself be seen, find the courage to be authentic, and let the world see the real you. Don't shy away from vulnerability, but rather embrace it. Being vulnerable is something to be proud of, for it shows that you are alive and willing to evolve and become a better person.

ALIGNING with your SELF

In a world led by ego where people are always competing and looking for ways to outdo one another, it is easy to become caught up in competitiveness and learn to think little of ourselves. When we find no other way to measure success than by mirroring our lives to others, we fail to see the beauty in what we accomplish. For optimal happiness and fulfillment, it is primordial to stay true to oneself; to align our thoughts and actions with all facets of our being. You will find that no matter how many times the world leads you astray, the best version of yourself lies within you.

"Knowing others is intelligence; knowing yourself is true wisdom. Mastering others is strength; mastering yourself is true power."

— TAO TE CHING

ALIGNING with ourselves is not a difficult thing to do, but often we get in the way of our true expression by suffocating who we are in an attempt to please others or conform to societal norms. We give in on things we should not compromise because we are afraid. We allow outside influences to dictate the parameters of our being and our existence. When we live like this, things that would naturally come to us are lost in the process of trying so hard to fit in.

The truth is, there is and will always be an infinite amount of ways in which to better ourselves. Perfection is an illusion, so why sacrifice unique parts of your making to fit a different mold? Forget inadequacy, incompleteness, and unworthiness. We are all born complete, with a fully-equipped toolbox; the time has come to learn how to use these tools.

On a final note, there are several ways in which you can learn to release old energies, fear-induced toxic patterns, long-ingrained insecurities fuelled by out-dated beliefs, self-destructive thoughts, and harmful attachments. Speaking to a therapist or a mental health specialist is often a catalyst to diving into yourself and re-aligning with who you are. Seeking help to better oneself is a powerful act of strength and courage.

Establishing boundaries

Once you've been able to get a grip on outside influences and have begun the process of defining your values, the next step would be to seek ways in which to establish where you stand and determine what you are willing to let in. As you learn to take responsibility for your thoughts and actions and their outcomes, setting emotional and social boundaries becomes vital in cultivating your sense of self in relation to others. They support you in gaining a sense of control over your actions, feelings, and physical space. Boundaries should reflect the outcome of a deep-seated personal value system. They dictate what you accept into your life and what you chose to dismiss for lack of service to yourself.

To create proper boundaries, you need to know as much as you can about yourself. That means knowing what is of high importance to you and pinpointing things that do not serve you. It is defining what is negotiable and what is not acceptable. Going through this process will allow you to get in touch with your emotions, beliefs, ideas, and feelings and teach you to sit comfortably with them. This developed inner intimacy helps you correctly measure the things you can and cannot accommodate, in other words, where you draw the line.

No one can know you better than you know yourself. This simple fact puts you in the best position to lead this journey. As you navigate the waters of growing into yourself, you will come to build self-reliance and hold yourself accountable for all your actions. Within your boundaries, people will come to understand what to expect, thus creating a natural process of eliminating the unwanted. As you begin to clearly state what is permitted within your space, all of which no longer serves your purpose will come to diverge into inexistence.

OWN YOUR TRUTH. Your experiences, mistakes, successes, and failures define not only who you are but also shape who you become, so don't be afraid to greet the package deal with open arms. You cannot expect to be held in high esteem if your self-respect is not established through principled goals and values and defined by clear boundaries. Work your way inwards, towards a place of acceptance. Welcome your flaws as a part of the whole unique entity that is your being.

3

LISTENING TO YOUR SOUL

> ""As I began to love myself, I recognized that my mind can disturb me and it can make me sick. But as I connected it to my heart, my mind became a valuable ally. Today I call this connection WISDOM OF THE HEART"

> — CHARLIE CHAPLIN

HUMAN BEINGS ARE MORE than just muscles, bones, and blood. We possess a non-physical omnipresent component, one that most of us know little about. This aspect of the individual is known as the soul. The soul is, in part, responsible for the intricate workings of the mind and designated personality attributes. It is made up of mental abilities such as reason, character, consciousness, feeling, memory, thinking, perception, etc. The workings of the soul can be complicated and abstract. Most importantly, the soul is an aspect of the human make-up, which is the seat of our intuition, the inner self.

The soul has its own voice and is ever speaking to us through various means like feelings, sensations, and thoughts. We all have the power to receive this intuitive guidance from our inside but certain factors like overpowering emotional responses, stress, strong beliefs, etc. have a way of distorting the download of this information or message.

Unfortunately, the experience most of us have here on Earth has created a distancing with something that was once familiar to us at a soul level. Our life path and the lessons we encounter, if interpreted as such, can be viewed as an attempt to drive us back to what needs to make us true to ourselves and allow us to reconnect to our inner selves.

It is not easy to listen to and make sense of the messages being processed continuously through our system and demanding our inner self's attention. However, there are some tools and exercises at our disposal that can allow for a smooth download of information from our inner self so that we may claim back our power with an authentic twist.

Accessing your higher-self

Many of us have been in situations where we just know things even before obtaining tangible evidence of these happenings. Cases such as the betrayal of a loved one often seem to bring their lot of forewarning signs, whether we acknowledge their worth or dismiss them for fear of uncovering the truth. They are often unexplainable. It may be difficult to persuade others – let alone ourselves – that these signs are valid, as we often lack tangible evidence to support our convictions and claims.

Varying according to personal beliefs, intuitive hunches may be explained in many ways. About ten years ago, I recall a day when I first heard that clear yet subtle voice in my head. I was dating this man I had known for a short period. We were walking down a riverbank on a warm, sunny summer's day. It was romantic and comfortable, and I felt quite content. Yet somehow, out of nowhere, this voice echoed through my mind: "*Run*. Run away *now*." Now, I can assure you that this was not a motivational slogan to incite me to take on a fitness regimen (I was actually quite fit at that point in time); however, this clear, loud voice turned out to be an accurate signal. That relationship was doomed to fail, and when I think back on it now, I feel quite lucky that it ended early rather than later. Perhaps it was my higher-self, maybe my intuition. Spiritually speaking, some may be convinced beyond doubt that spirit guides were protecting me. Whichever option appeals most to you, we must reach the consensus that there is a wiser, higher guidance than our conscious way of living within society permits us to see. Let's take a further look into the concept of listening to your soul.

WHAT EXACTLY IS this concept of higher self? Well, simply put, it is the *real* you. It is an intrinsic part of your make-up and is ever communicating with you. It oversees your life and can grasp things that are not within your reach, as it is fundamentally unbiased and non-judgmental. Your higher self can process things you cannot grasp, for the physical body does not limit it within the restricted space of your tangible reality. It is a part of you that you can tame and learn to connect in order to expand your consciousness and gain a different perspective. When we say "only you know what's best," your higher self is, in fact, the all-knowing genius. Tapping into your higher self can guide and heal you in so many ways. It is the part of us that is wise beyond measure and unaffected by the sequence of positive or negative happenings in our lives.

The higher self is linked to innate wisdom and creativity and is not a product of our conscious mind. Think of all the dormant potential that lies within you. How beautiful would it be if we could tap into such unique insights? The truth is, we can and we will.

How can we access this higher self and increase the frequency in which we connect to it? As we've said, it is a part of us that is ever communicating. Still, we have become so accustomed to perceiving and experiencing through our physical senses that we've come to ignore this fundamental non-physical part of us. There are several ways through which we can connect with our higher self. Most of these methods are easily accessible, such as meditation (observing and detaching from thoughts), mindfulness (or mindlessness, if you prefer), exercise and play, creative expression, acknowledging your instincts, and harnessing your talents and gifts.

How to communicate with your higher self

The higher self is ever communicating, and it does so through various means such as dreams, gut feelings, intuitive hunches, and insights. We are continually connected to this source; our role is to be sensitive enough to pick up inner cues to lead us towards the best path to benefit our growth and development. These signals can be in the form of a funny feeling in the pit of your stomach, sweaty palms, or an unexplainable certainty that something is not as it should be. Let's look at some of the ways our higher self is communicating with us.

GUT FEELING

This is also known as gut instinct or intuition. It is a visceral knowing, beyond all reason and tangible evidence. You just know that something isn't right, even though you can't explain it. This knowledge is not derived from a conscious level but rather an intuitive one. Perhaps the entrance of a person into a room can cause you to sense a certain unusual energy; at times, you may feel a flow of positive energy upon meeting a person. Other times it may express itself as palpable tension in the air. We can sense these things as our instinct kicks in, even before our conscious mental faculties can make sense of them.

This gut instinct comes up as a feeling from within you, and only you can experience it. Since this feeling is personal, only you can tell how it feels, and conclude with your own interpretation. This is why only you can decide to listen to and follow your intuition. Acknowledging your gut feeling is a sign of trusting yourself.

Try picturing this. You've recently gone through a difficult break-up and separation from your (now ex) spouse. The end of the relationship was tumultuous. It has been a long and painful process, but you are finally beginning to feel free from the hold of your ex's toxic grip.

One day, you are feeling unwell at work. Deciding to head home to catch up on some much-needed rest, you arrive at your house earlier than usual that afternoon. As you pull into the driveway, you get a strange feeling of unease. You look around, but everything looks normal; you assume everything is normal and head for the front door. Finding your keys at the bottom of your work bag, you unlock the door and step into the house. The familiar space is welcoming; however, an uneasy feeling consumes you, reaching the pit of your stomach and squeezing into your chest. It is difficult to pinpoint, but as you turn around and notice the open window that you had shut before going to work, the familiar odor in the air brings clarity. At once, the image of your ex fills your mind's eye, and understanding sets in: you know, without a doubt, that he is in the house.

This scenario is not uncommon, and it is one example that shows how our instincts can help process all that happens around us. Whether or not you are an observant person, it is impossible to grasp every detail, every happening in our daily surroundings. However, we have a way of taking in information on a subconscious level. Sometimes it manifests itself emotionally or physically, at times without being able to identify the source consciously. We know, but we don't understand how or why. Our subconscious mind, which is also the source of dreams and storage of unresolved issues, influences our thoughts and feelings and ensures that we respond to our environment as per our programmed self.

Whatever you deduced regarding the origin of the odor in the house, it was an obvious trigger to previously suppressed thoughts – in this case, the unpleasantness of a painful separation – and might have been the residue of your ex's perfume floating in the air. Perhaps there was an extra pair of shoes in the hallway, one that you hadn't consciously taken notice of, but that your brain had associated with memories of a shared life, creating an emotional reaction.

Charlie Chaplin once said: "As I began to love myself, I found that anguish and emotional suffering are only warning signs that I am living against my own truth." Bearing this in mind, we can now make a connection between gut instinct or intuition and living authentically. Authenticity is vital, and it is a powerful game-changer. If listened to and nurtured, intuition and instinct can be enhanced and reveal many inner-truths, intensifying our daily life experience.

INTUITIVE HUNCHES

Intuitive hunches occur when you feel subtle nudges to do or say something. We all have experienced these inner cues to visit a particular place, stay at home, attend an event, meet someone, or avoid a person. These nudges are ways through which your higher self communicates and guides you to a better path.

Now, I will say this: the higher self is always right. It is meant to be a guide, and it is competently doing that job. The only problem comes from the place of downloading the information and transferring it to the mind. This information, whether received as an intuition, dream, insight, or a hunch, in its purest form, can be interpreted in a number of ways. Although it is an untainted part of your awareness at the source, it can become diluted with your emotions and thoughts and distorted into misinterpretation. However, with practice, you can improve your mode of access and quality of download of this information. Developing your ability to focus and clear your mind, observing your environment, and responding unbiasedly, improving impartial thought-observation through practices like meditation, mindfulness can be highly beneficial in connecting to your essence. Additionally, learning to identify and separate wishful thinking from real gut feeling or insights is a fundamental part of the process.

. . .

Thoughts vs. reality

As the common iceberg analogy goes, our mind operates in ways that allow merely a glimpse of what is at the surface of its workings. There is so much more hidden out of sight: countless concepts beyond our reach and notions we cannot grasp. Our thoughts float about, in and out of the surface of our mind, and are mere representations of every component of our existence. Thoughts are affected by several factors, such as emotions, upbringing, personal beliefs, and much more. Just as the top level of the iceberg, perhaps 10% of its entire composition, is apparent above sea level, your conscious thoughts are only a minor part of the workings of your mind. There is so much information that we take in without processing, and most of what does appear in our train of thoughts does not particularly serve us.

With the practice of mindfulness and meditation, you can come to patiently observe your thoughts as they make their way through, witnessing them from an unbiased and non-judgmental perspective. In a world where we are continually overstimulated, overburdened, and under constant pressure, this process can decrease unnecessary information upload that often generates emotional responses. This process takes time and regular practice; it is a habit to develop for long-term benefits. Most of us are not conditioned to be observers of our thoughts; instead, we are taught to respond to our environment by immediate reactions and raising shields driven by one's ego. Staying in tune with your thought patterns can eventually alter your protective mechanisms and help you go through life with a much lighter load on your shoulders.

At this point, you might want to take a moment to pause.

Close your eyes if you need to. Take a few deep breaths. At this point, can you differentiate your perceptions from the actual, factual circumstances to which you are prone to react? You may want to look back on the last 24 to 48 hours of your life. Everything you did, from grocery shopping to parking the car, from minding for loved-ones to answering emails, could have been a trigger. In fact, it often is. Many daily misinterpretations lead us to react negatively, which harms us more than we can imagine.

Your subconscious mind is processing every sensation and experience that goes through your mind every moment of the day – this being the 90% of the iceberg underwater. Everything that you've experienced since the day you were born is kept in this enormous vault. This reservoir will continue to receive and store experiences until your last breath. By taking action and altering your conscious thought patterns, you are filtering the quality of information that will be stored subconsciously, as your subconscious responds to your already established behavioral patterns.

Only a fraction of your experiences and knowledge can be accessed while the rest are hidden away in your subconscious mind. When you experience emotional reactivity episodes with physical symptoms such as sweaty palms, an uneasy feeling, or knowing something before actually knowing it, your intuition is trying to download information from your subconscious into your conscious mind. Your subconscious accesses the stored knowledge and experiences and uses them to help you make sense of situations to preserve or keep you safe. It works on autopilot, mostly helping you view and interpret reality through the way in which you were conditioned.

On the other hand, your thoughts come from your conscious mind and are not real, but only your interpretation of reality. The truth is, even if you spend all your time thinking about something, it will not alter what it is. Stressing about a job interview and overthinking all that could go wrong will not change the outcome. All the energy you've put into focusing on fabulation sacrifices clarity, focus, and productivity.

Your thoughts are not your actual reality. They are and always will be a representation, and therefore it is within your power to alter their impact on your body and emotional responses. Sitting in silence, even for five minutes every day, and observing the flow of your imagination, may be a very impactful method to gain more connection to your thought patterns and to yourself.

Prioritizing self-respect

Standing your ground and refusing to follow the crowd can be extremely daunting. It leaves us in a highly vulnerable state, as it is part of our making to seek acceptance and belonging. When we have spent a large chunk of our lives people-pleasing, it can be quite challenging to speak freely and act as we please.

Knowing your priorities and respecting your individuality can be a challenging concept to implement, as you might struggle with not seeking outside validation and gratification. Establishing clear-cut boundaries through knowing your values and priorities can help make sense of where you stand and where you should draw the line. This will allow you to focus on what matters most to you.

Doing all these things can only happen once you have clearly defined what is most important to you. When you do, it becomes easier to respect your needs and wants and speak your mind, rather than ignoring or suppressing them. This is not only crucial for your sanity but can also impact your general health and wellbeing.

The capacity to make authentic and life-defining decisions is mainly dependent on what your priorities are. Priorities and personal values serve as a toolkit with which you can better understand yourself, and they are those upon which you rely to set healthy boundaries. As you learn to do this, it will lead to clarity about who you are, your values, and the best way to approach life.

What does knowing your priorities and respecting your wants and needs look like?

- It implies being honest enough to recognize what you most need and commit to acknowledging rather than dismissing them.
- It is being unapologetic and direct when it comes to making your priorities known to yourself and others. In other words: creating *boundaries*.
- It is knowing that having unique needs and wants is perfectly normal.
- It is being able to take responsibility for your actions.
- It is having a growth-mindset and expecting favorable outcomes.

YOUR VALUES ARE one of the most essential factors in your life. They form the support structure of your life. Your values determine what you accept or reject as part of your existence. They define the choices you make, and these choices then determine the direction of your life. Our values should influence all of our decisions. Stick to your core values and listen to your heart.

Many of us disconnectedly navigate life, suppressing our innermost needs and desires. It is instilled in us from an early age to accept our carers' rules and values and our upbringing's social model. There comes a point in our lives when we must decide if we wish to continue down that path or step away from conventions and get to know our true selves. Until you define the rules by which you want to live and experience life, you are simply not living authentically. You are a prisoner of your shadow until you claim yourself back, taking hold of all that is truly important to you, values, and actions mirroring your soul and reflecting your heart.

At this point, the values transferred to you during your upbringing matter very little, nor does it matter which values are directing your current life choices. Understand that having clearly defined personal values is how you show respect to yourself. The only values that matter are the ones that can bring you happiness, meaning, fulfillment, connection and success in life are your core values, the non-negotiable ties to the deepest part of your heart and soul.

Take some time to determine what invigorates you, what makes you want to get out of bed every morning. I'm sure you've heard this before, but have you ever actually tried? Have you ever stopped to contemplate what may be your soul's calling, however accessible, possible, or out of reach it might seem to be? What is it that you would happily lose sleep over, what is it that you want to be remembered for? What brings an instant smile to your face and colors your life and that of others?

One other thing. Values are not written in stone; just as you are continually striving to become a more balanced person, your values are subject to change. What matters most is that these values which influence and guide your life come from you and are not what others determine is "right." As you evolve and grow through challenges and adversity, your values may need to be realigned, which is more than fine. Allow yourself to test the waters of existence, to improve, and strive to become a better person. Seize the moment, and grasp those opportunities. Don't let yourself be the one to stand in your way.

LASTLY, no one can dictate your path if you do not allow them to do so. Your truth is your identity, and no one can deny you this power unless you give it away. Know your priorities, define your boundaries while respecting those of others, and see yourself become a more authentic version of yourself.

RELEASE & connect through sharing

Life as we know it is not one linear line. It has its thrills, stresses, pains, and pleasures. It is full of influential factors such as work, family, politics, and societal expectations that can burden our emotional state, just as they can excite and thrill us. Added to them are the ever-increasing pressures of relationships, technology, beauty, and fashion (to name a few), all of which can leave us in a position of mental struggle.

When we are faced with these challenging situations, our actions and reactions are expressed in the form of emotions. These emotional responses can range from anger to shame, from fear to confusion, happiness, sadness, and loneliness, just to name a few. These emotions are powerful, and most are an overpowering part of our lives because they are how we view and interpret our reality.

Being a significant part of our everyday experience, emotions must be handled carefully and healthily, or we will fail to reap its attendant benefits. Feelings are normal and healthy, so they should not be ignored, suppressed, or treated with disdain. They are to be thoughtfully responded to and dealt with adequately. There are very healthy and efficient means of dealing with emotions, whether negative or positive. A productive way of doing this is through talk therapy.

Talk therapy, also known as psychotherapy or counselling, is founded on the basic idea of talking through emotions to put them into perspective. This approach is also useful in treating other issues such as depression, chronic stress, anxiety, etc. The primary goal of any therapy is helping patients to better deal with their life situations. This system, usually beginning with seeking out a professional therapist, provides a suitable means to connect with your emotions and release them.

As SAID ABOVE, there is always a better way to handle emotions other than ignoring, drowning, or suppressing them. Suppose the chosen method to deal with emotions fails to address the situation adequately. In that case, it will only lead to the perpetuation of whatever it is you're trying to avoid in the first place. Any method that is not the right way of dealing with these emotions can create suffering and prevent you from living fully. A reliable, time-tested means of dealing correctly with these emotions is through mindfulness.

As per Oxford Dictionary, mindfulness is defined as "a

mental state achieved by concentrating on the present moment, while calmly accepting the feelings and thoughts that come to you, used as a technique to help you relax." Mindfulness can be seen as a meditative state, through which you focus on paying attention to specific aspects of your surroundings or dive inwards and pay attention to your breathing. It may involve doing a body scan, which allows you to entirely drop into the present moment and notice how every single part of you is feeling. Perhaps if you stop and listen, you'll hear a bird chirping, or discover a faint smell of freshly mown grass, or even observe a cloud that looks surprisingly like your uncle Fred.

MINDFULNESS IS all about being present in the moment and tuning in with yourself. With short bouts of regular practice, it can turn negative emotions (anger, grief, anxiety, embarrassment, remorse) into a neutral emotional state. Transitioning into acceptance, these can become important sources of strength and wisdom. How is this possible? Regular mindfulness practices can alter how we view and react to these emotions. It is by turning towards these emotions, facing them, accepting them, and releasing them once they have served their purpose. As the wise Eckhart Tolle has said, "Whatever you fight, you strengthen, and what you resist, persists." It is crucial to our personal development to learn to lean into discomfort; "Trying to feel the feelings, staying mindful about numbing behaviors, trying to lean into the discomfort of hard emotions" (Brown, 2010). Dr. Brown goes on to add that "we cannot selectively numb emotions. When we numb the painful emotions, we also numb the positive emotions." If you can find the strength to feel your way through vulnerable experiences mindfully, you will discover a much deeper connection to your true self and build your strength of character and resilience.

MINDFULNESS ALLOWS FOR KIND, compassionate, caring, and patient attention to whatever you're going through. It is a means of regulating emotions and connecting to your authentic self. Below is a sequence of steps to help in dealing with challenging emotions mindfully. It is a process I learned as a young adult and have used it successfully many times over the years. In this technique, visualization is key.

1. **Noticing**

Noticing is the art of mindful observation. It is the initial state during which you feel the emotional response in your body, sometimes manifesting itself through tears, stomach pain, skin rashes, tightness in the chest, sweaty palms, and more. The first step to begin dealing with these emotions is to notice them. Pause for a moment, take a deep breath, sit with the guilt, shame, anger, fear, frustration, or anxiety, and observe them without judgment. Avoid inhibiting, ignoring, or suppressing these emotions. Simply notice and entertain them with an attitude of acceptance and open curiosity.

2. **Identifying**

After you've spent a moment observing your emotions, you should now identify what they are. You may wish to verbalize what the feelings are; this creates a sense of lightness and makes you consciously aware of what you feel. Begin with statements such as "I feel anger" or "I feel sadness," while visualizing the area in your body where you feel this emotion. You should avoid statements such as "I am angry," as they personify emotions. You are not your emotion, nor does it possess you. Using the former statements is powerful, as it allows simultaneous detachment and empowerment. You are permitting yourself to feel this way. It is a form of self-compassion and opens-up a gateway towards the next step.

3. Accepting

Imagine you are greeting a long-lost friend with open arms. That is precisely the way you should approach your emotional response. It serves you for a higher purpose; it is part of your making and a sign of vitality. Accepting your emotion implies feeding it love. I like to picture myself cradling the emotion as I would an infant. While this may sound strange, it is a potent tool in releasing negativity. When you are capable of embracing the parts of yourself that you would usually suppress, everything shifts. You are now feeding yourself pure, non-judgmental, untainted love. Acceptance is a significant step in the process of letting go.

4. Releasing

"To let go does not mean to get rid of. To let go means to let be. When we let be with compassion, things come and go on their own." (Kornfield, 2008)

After accepting your emotions and feeding them love, the next step is to let them go. At this point, you will have created a distance between yourself and these feelings, so all that is left to do is to release them.

To do so, I suggest you use another visualization technique. When you feel ready, as you hold your pain, you will choose to send it back out of yourself and direct it into the universe. This is one of many ways; it is a very personal process, and you must choose a method through which you feel comfortable. Like everything else, practice makes perfect. The more you practice visualizing, the easier it will become.

NOW THAT WE have covered this four-step process, you are better equipped to be mindfully accepting of your emotions. Go ahead and hold them in your awareness, sprinkling them with some much-needed TLC. This alone will help to soothe and calm you, as it is also a meditative process. Ultimately, it helps create somewhat of a mental space around emotional responses, making it possible for you to witness from a distance instead of struggling through a state of tumult.

AS WE FUNCTION through a limited perspective of life and all that is possible, it is beyond our conscious ability to see the invisible. One of our largest and most impactful misconceptions is that we assume that all others think the way we do. As such, it has been said that no one sees what you see, even if they see it too. Sit with yourself and take notice of your inner-voice; connect to your soul. Can you reach outside this paradigm and listen to your higher self?

CONNECT WITH YOUR INNER CHILD

> "Each one of us has an inner child, or way of being. Getting in touch with your inner child can help foster well-being and bring lightness to life."
>
> — Dr Diana Raab

Before diving into this topic, let's go over the concept of the inner child. Your inner child is an innate aspect of yourself that paints the picture of the "little you." This metaphorical child is the source of all childhood memories. It is at once your innocence, the untainted and pure being that you once were, full of wonder and unhindered by societal barriers. This inner child experienced all of your earliest emotional traumas and comforts, as well as the numerous memories that came with them. Some still live at the surface of your mind; others, as a means of self-preservation, have been long-buried into your subconscious. Although they have yet to be resurrected, these experiences still significantly impact your everyday take on life. They come to shape our emotional responses and influence our decision-making process. It is clear to see why the inner child is the foundation of who we are today, the lens through which we perceive and respond to our world.

In the same way that a healthy child can be fun, playful, and resilient, a traumatized or injured child might develop a challenging adult life, particularly when his or her adult life experiences trigger the reappearance of buried past wounds.

Everyone has wounds. Bitter, painful, or unpleasant experiences often remain tied to our inner child. Whether we dare to admit it or not, the fact remains that our sensitive and vulnerable inner child yearns for love and approval. If it was not received then, we will still crave it now. Without healing, you will find yourself continually transferring those past wounds to your life today, most likely amplifying the consequences as you go. Whether the source of the emotional scars can be traced to psychological or physical abuse, a broken family, or the loss of a loved one, the resulting pain will be attached to us for all our lives; and we can be reminded of this anytime, anywhere. Traumatic experiences cannot be undone, but healing from these wounds is possible.

When we connect to our inner child, we can access information that will make us understand some of the frequent obstacles we face, such as negative patterns that impair our self-development and self-actualization. It is possible to uncover the unhealed wounds, what is responsible for them, and how we can heal those wounds, on a profound level, so that we can live in our world of today as well-rounded adults. This connection can bring about in-depth healing and lead to the transformation of our lives.

Below are some strategies that can help connect to your inner child so that you can heal and experience the best that life has to offer.

Forgive yourself

We may want to deny it, but the fact remains that our past stays with us. Dreams are a standard gateway for repressed memories or past events to resurface. Our past often finds a way to replay itself in our present, and in doing so, influence our future. The past is who you were, today is who you are, and tomorrow is who you will be. You must understand that all of these aspects are intrinsically connected; therefore, altering one will influence the others. Ask yourself this question: which of these is within your control? How can you change one aspect to shift the direction of your life?

Many of us have this firm belief that holding onto past mistakes is unfavorable. Yet, many of us repeat said mistakes because we do not know how to free ourselves from this vicious cycle. The thing is until you shift your perspective, you will continue to be held back by the hurt, pain, and negativity of yesterday. To start healing from past wounds and put yourself on the right path for the life of today, you must face your past head-on. Speaking to a specialist is often a powerful starting point. Sit in your discomfort, deal with our pain, heal your wounds. Treat them kindly and respectfully, for they are the foundation of your making. And you will *know* when you are ready to move forward. Your inner child will be free. You will move freely towards your future and back into your true self.

Yes, your upbringing might have been a less than perfect one, and your caregivers, parents, or guardians may have let you down on several grounds. But one thing you must come to terms with – and this will help you deal with the problem – is the fact that they are after all human, thus inevitably prone to mistakes. Remind yourself of this regularly to avoid empowering your past. If it is not beneficial to your self-development, what is done should be left behind you. Understand that blame doesn't help anyone, and it certainly does not serve you.

Obviously, merely being aware of this fact will not make your trauma or pain magically disappear. Yet, one of the things it will do for you is to prevent past wounds from festering. Holding on to the ugliness of your past for too long can lead you to the point where you harbor resentment, are held captive by your own pain and abide by a victim mentality.

This is when you should consider connecting to your inner child to help you correctly manage the situation. Doing so may give you insight and lead you to recognize that your emotions are possibly a derivation of your past challenges. We sometimes react from a childlike perspective when confronted with unresolved issues from our upbringing, these of which often result in emotional insecurities. Your inner child is ever-present, but he is not who you are today. You have the power to determine what should stay in your past and what belongs to your present and will serve you in the future.

I urge you to tackle unresolved issues headfirst and avoid

dwelling on your past: your upbringing, the circumstances of your childhood, your successes, and failures. Dwelling on what is done is like bathing in your filth, day after day; it is uncomfortable, messy, and offers no positive outcome. It is unhelpful and will hold you in the grip of longing and despair. Furthermore, it will serve you to no extent, merely hindering your ability to progress and move forward on your journey. Sure, it will take courage to remove yourself from the grasp of self-pity. Pull that plug and drain that tainted water; it is time to refill and cleanse. Believe me when I say this: the temporary discomfort of facing your past will be well worth the opportunities that await you on the other side.

Give yourself permission to be flawed

COGNITIVE DISTORTIONS

The human brain is wired to control movement, sensations, and thoughts. I am not suggesting that we ignore or second guess what our brain tells us every time, but there are instances where second-guessing instinctive reactions may be of great benefit. Your brain may have developed some unhelpful connections over time. You will be surprised to discover how common it is to make non-existent connections between ideas and thoughts. This tendency of the brain to make faulty connections is the foundation of cognitive distortions.

So, what are cognitive distortions? Essentially, they are thought patterns that alter our perception of reality. Moreover, they are usually negatively biased. What does this mean? It implies that we often inhibit our potential by the means of automated negative thought patterns. It is one of our many coping mechanisms and is a common way of dealing with adversity.

Often unreasonable and illogical, these beliefs and thoughts unknowingly become reinforced over time. The thing about these types of thought patterns - and the reason we need to be aware of them - is that they are very subtle and difficult to recognize, even (especially) when they are a regular occurrence. Cognitive distortions come in different forms, such as emotional reasoning, overgeneralizing, filtering, jumping to conclusions, catastrophizing, etc. and have the following thing in common: they are inaccurate or false patterns of thinking that have the potential to cause psychological damage.

Many of us are quick to point out that we cannot be held down by distorted thoughts or fall prey to them, but the truth is, complete denial makes us even more vulnerable to these destructive beliefs. The goal is not to avoid these thought patterns at all costs but rather to acknowledge them and reflect on how they impact our lives.

Let me show you how easily we can get caught up in cognitive distortions.

We all view ourselves in a particular way, often projecting to the world a version of us that we want others to see in order to be accepted. Knowing that this image that we have created for ourselves makes us feel valued by people and puts us in a dignified position, we tend to keep it up, and even when this person we have created no longer exists, we pretend to stick to that personae.

As time goes by, extra layers are added to this image so

that our flawless appearance continues to be seen as perfect. This leads to a situation where we are unable to relate appropriately with people because we're afraid to let them see our flaws. Our private life may be a mess, and we may be unhappy because our life revolves around living up to the personae that we think others expect. Just like Jim Carrey's character in *The Mask*, you may slowly mold into the person you are projecting to others while neglecting your true self.

If we are not ready to accept the fact that we are not the perfect person we say or let people think we are, it becomes challenging to come to terms with our imperfections. In trying to defend our position, we may begin to blame our friends, the weather, fate, or our background for any perceived flaw instead of simply accepting the fact that it's okay not to be perfect. As a result, we harbor false and illogical beliefs, drawing conclusions where none exists and making irrational generalizations. Here are some examples of such cognitive distortions:

- *I must be perfect or seen to be perfect*
- *Some people are perfect*
- *It is a sign of weakness to accept that I am flawed or imperfect*
- *People will hate me if they find out I'm not perfect*
- *I am stupid, and that is why my partner left me*
- *I am the unluckiest person in the whole world*
- *I couldn't even do that; I'm never going to amount to much in life*

There are endless examples of cognitive distortions where people interpret their reality in inaccurate and often negative ways. They become overwhelmed by this flawed thought process and will begin to interpret circumstances through feelings.

There are many ways to go about undoing this kind of harmful thinking, the first one being to acknowledge those unhelpful thought patterns. As we've already discussed, talking to someone and sharing your concerns may help get things in motion. Repressed thoughts tend to resurface when we verbalize them. Also, coming to terms with the fact that you don't have to be perfect to live a happy, successful, and fulfilled life will allow for a truer, more authentic dialogue within yourself. Being flawed is part of human complexity (and who is to determine what should be considered a flaw, anyway?) and will not make you any less than you are. Welcome your weakness, as they are full of dormant potential. Being vulnerable has a way of drawing you closer to your true self. Allowing and embracing this perception will help you to deal with cognitive distortions effectively. It will give you permission to be you and the freedom to make mistakes, evolve, and grow. It is alright to be beautifully and perfectly flawed.

BREAK DOWN

Have you ever been in a situation where you just hate your life? You step back and take a look at who you've become, or how you are living, and you can tell that something is missing? Maybe you just have this feeling that this life you're living isn't yours. This is because your existence has been forged on the grounds and influence of others. Perhaps you have been trying to conform to a set of rules, norms, and expectations, and in doing so, you've neglected your true self. It is a common trait in most societies to abide by certain codes. We have all been, to some level, socially, emotionally, and mentally conditioned to live by the rules of others, to respond to the expectations of parents, spouses, friends, and family. In this process, our self-expression was most-likely inhibited. The constant struggle between acceptance of others and creating our own path can be overwhelmingly challenging. As a result, it is easy to lose control of our life, to lose our sense of purpose, and ultimately have no idea who to be and how to live a life that is truly ours.

As a young child, you were undoubtedly free-spirited. You probably loved to visit the back of the house and play in the dirt; maybe you enjoyed talking to animals and creating fantasy worlds where you could stay for hours. You were infinitely curious and wanted to understand every single aspect of your environment.

In becoming the adult you are now, you most likely had to take apart the person you were many years ago. Social conventions and expectations tend to dictate how we progress through those teenage years, and as the habits solidify, they keep hold of us as we enter adulthood. We learn when to speak and when to be quiet. We are taught exactly how to act to gain others' approval, which is often perceived as a means to success. We may stop questioning for fear of being wrong or, worse, for holding absolute certainty that we have full knowledge of all there is.

As a direct result of your response to societal rules, how you express yourself is derived by how you perceive yourself within your environment and forms the foundation of who you are. Although there can be many barriers to self-expression, it is one of the ways in which you project your personality by sharing ideas and communicating thoughts. Self-expression is the way we express or make ourselves known.

There are many ways through which you can express your authentic self. It can take various forms, some of which are talking (verbal or non-verbal), facial expressions, body movements, actions, and physical appearance. When your manner of expression is interrupted, corrupted, or weakened by anyone in any way, it can set the tone for who you become for the rest of your life. Healthy self-expression is a vital part of your life and wellbeing. The journey of self-discovery can be seen by some cultures as selfish, unusual, odd. Unfortunately, it can even be perceived as a time-wasting endeavor, but the truth is that self-expression is of great importance in society. If no one speaks their mind and everyone acts the same, there is no room for change and evolution. In fact, "the journey of self-discovery is the most important journey we can take" (De la Huerta, 2014). Self-expression provides a platform for us to be ourselves, attain fulfillment, and contribute richly to our world.

Genuine and authentic self-expression is how we embrace who we are, whether it be the positive traits that we proudly expose or the dark and less valued parts that we are quick to hide away. Apart from the fact that true self-expression encourages us to be our best, it creates room for us to work more effectively with others (Glaser, 2016). Through self-expression, we can move away from our protection mechanisms and eventually begin to open up to others.

Many of us are stuck in his situation. We may be seen to be doing well, but the truth is that our life is full of fears, self-doubt, low self-esteem, and shame. It's time to breakdown these barriers; it's time to be truly YOU. Choose to reclaim passion for your life.

No one knows you better than you know yourself. No one but you can and should choose how you live your life. It's time to go back to who you were when it all started, to the place where you feel whole.

Perhaps the time has come to break down the multiple

layers of your fake façade, the one you have been cultivating since your first breath. Who was there before it all, before norms, rules, and expectations? What is the essence of your soul?

UNBURY POTENTIAL

IN THE LATE 1960s, NASA developed a series of tests regarding sources of creativity, innovation, and imaginative ability. They were hoping to discover whether these factors are inborn, learned, or acquired by experience. These extensive experiments led to the conclusion that it is not that children lose the ability to be creative, but that it is taught out of them. The data collected showed that our school system's education robs us of our innovative, creative, explorative, and imaginative genius.

As children, we were naturally curious about the world and always eager to know why things are the way they are. We loved to freely explore our environment, being instinctively intuitive and perceptive, and paying attention to the little things. These attributes and others are an essential part of what makes children highly innovative and creative. The traditional schooling system, teaching us how to behave in society, can come to repress many of these natural tendencies. School is, for the most part, a place of conformity. And although many educators try their best to allow kids to remain as they are, the school system does not concede enough space for individuals to strive for uniqueness. It has slowly and progressively erased them while dumbing down in the process.

According to researcher Judith Glaser, the state of our

inner child is where we are most innovative. She states that when we align with our true self, our inner self, a part of our brain known as the prefrontal cortex is activated, thereby granting us higher access to abilities such as innovative and creative thinking, planning, and problem-solving. This is one more reason why we should seek to reconnect with our inner child.

Take time to cultivate your inner child, get involved in things that will set your soul on fire, and by so doing, provide yourself with the needed opportunity to free yourself from any dumbing down that years of education and schooling has done on you. Tap into your inner child to create, invent, explore, and innovate. Give yourself the liberty to be your true self again.

EMERGENCE

Think about this: What are the things that naturally make you laugh? What is a sure way to turn your frown upside down? What thoughts bring you tears of joy? What memories make your heart glow?

We all have some wonderful memories of when we were little. A time when we would endlessly jump on the bed, throw pillows, and cover our faces with our underwear, a time of pure, fresh, and renewed interaction with our surroundings. Those were moments of play, moments where we had no worries in our minds, moments of unlimited fun, and pure bliss.

So much has happened between then and now that we have forgotten about those moments of wild and unbridled laughter, smiles, and joy. The infinite demands of adulthood can subtly take over what used to be silliness and careless-

ness. Endless time-consuming demands keep us discon-
nected from our inner-child.

Some people are ever bothered by this change; it can be
seen as the natural order of things, so they are not perturbed.
Some believe childhood is the time to play, and when that
time comes to pass, we must move on and focus on making
the right choices and being responsible. The question is, have
we truly outgrown our inner-child?

What if we were to hold on to some of the beloved
aspects of our little selves and watch as they flourish into
adulthood? You can try to recall what defined you as a
person before becoming an adult or even before your
teenage years. What soothed you, and what made you react?
Who were your friends, and what kind of person did you
enjoy spending time with? This is not to say that we must
not evolve; all the opposite. We do often outgrow places and
people. Such is life. However, if you can reach back to a time
before all the societal grooming and conditioning, back to
when you were unburdened by the worries of this world, you
may tap into the innocence of your soul and your true
essence.

Next time you are faced with an unpalatable situation,
reconnect with your inner child; remember those things that
naturally make you laugh and smile; those thoughts that
bring you tears of joy, and those memories that make your
heart glow.

Reclaim and take advantage of the power of your inner
child by finding activities that your inner child loves and get
involved in them. Whatever it is that you truly enjoy and that
brings the best out of you, explore it. Reach for everything
that sets your soul on fire: create, invent, explore, and innovate. Try things that scare you, step out of your comfort
zone, and you may just be surprised by the dormant poten-

tial you discover. Allow yourself uncomplicated moments of creativity and play, and liberate yourself from the ties of expectations.

Life is not as complicated as we make it out to be. The best you can do is learn from the authentic and spontaneous child you once were. Reconnect with your inner self, your inner child, and tap back into happiness, joy, and peace.

5

EMBRACING PATIENCE & UNCERTAINTY

~

"When you become comfortable with uncertainty, infinite possibilities open up in your life."

— ECKHART TOLLE

EXPERIMENTS CARRIED out about six decades ago revealed that when people have foreknowledge that they will be exposed to painful or discomforting situations, for example, an electric shock or an unpleasant image, they react far less than when they are exposed to these same conditions when they are not expecting it. This is due to the fact that uncertainty makes preparing for or controlling events difficult.

David Rock unveils some of the mechanisms of thought patterns in *Your Brain at Work*, in which he states that "the brain craves certainty. A sense of uncertainty about the future and feeling out of control both generate strong limbic system responses." (Rock, 2009) The limbic system, being (in part) responsible for emotional responses, is a powerful component of our make-up. Simply put, uncertainty tends to trigger adverse reactions. Being able to predict and anticipate events and our lives' happenings provide us with a sense of security. We are programmed to seek predictability to protect ourselves. Having to sit with the unknown, or losing a sense of direction, can provoke stress and anxiety as our minds struggle in coping with uncertainty.

According to researchers Dugas & Buhr (2009), "intolerance of uncertainty involves the tendency to react negatively on an emotional, cognitive, and behavioral level to uncertain situations and events." We are so afraid of not knowing what tomorrow may bring that this fear disrupts our long-term welfare and interferes with our emotional freedom.

In the time of our ancestors, who were majorly hunters and gatherers, some of the uncertainties they had to contend with were the threat of being killed by wild animals, attacks from rival tribal groups, harsh climatic conditions, and disease outbreak. Fortunately, we no longer face the same obstacles to our survival… but that doesn't exclude a renewed and updated set of existential uncertainties. So many aspects of our lives – important ones at that – are not within our control. We navigate unpredictable waters every day of our lives, unsure about the solidity of our relationships, the stability and growth of our finances, and the maintenance of our health; job security is not a given, nor is a stable political and economic climate. These elements are not easy to deal with, and if we cannot cope with being in a continuous state of uncertainty, it undoubtedly affects our mental health.

At the core of ourselves, we all are afraid of the future,

mainly because we do not know what lies ahead. We tend to assume that things will continue to be as they are. Only, none of us are immune to change or adversity. Whether it makes our lives take a turn for better or worse, the transitional state that is brought on by change tends to leave us in considerable discomfort.

Lacking confidence in our ability to cope with unexpected events or situations often leads to avoidance and suppressing emotions. The multiple repercussions of this include mind negativity bias, which is how our negative emotions take precedence over positive ones when confronted with a situation. This becomes a very harmful habit and is highly detrimental to our emotional and mental wellbeing.

Although we may believe we lack the necessary life skills to navigate uncertainty, we all possess the ability to choose how we respond. You hold the power to intercept your thoughts before they meet your emotions, and you possess the ability to prevent them from dissolving and spreading within your inner space. Whether you choose to believe your thoughts is entirely up to you. Remember that believing in your decisional power and stepping in and taking charge of your emotional responses is a substantial first step in the right direction.

Now, even though all humans are faced with the same problem of uncertainty, the way we react to it differs. Understand that these reactions are our coping mechanisms and our way of dealing with uncertainty. Those who resort to worrying are choosing to play it safe with risks and potential threats. Furthermore, in situations of uncertainty, one of the common ways in which we cope is to do something that we feel gives us an illusion of being in control, such as excessive planning, obsessive cleaning, dictating what others must do, and basically micro-managing every area of your life.

Now, developing resilience is a huge factor in learning to sit with uncertainty. Having complete faith in yourself and knowing that you possess the capacity to bounce back from adversity is full-proof. With this conviction, nothing can truly stand in your way. Whatever happens, you know yourself enough to trust in your resourcefulness.

Also, building up your tolerance to change and uncertainty by being willing to take risks and embrace discomfort can lead to a healthy way of coping. Hurdles will undoubtedly appear, but the more experience you have in facing them, the stronger you will be in meeting the challenges.

One sure thing about this world is its unavoidable and perilous uncertainty. No one knows what tomorrow holds. We cannot predict or control what others will do nor how others react. The best we can do is take steps to confront the fear of uncertainty.

HOW TO FACE uncertainty

Now, even though we know that allowing ourselves to feel our emotions - including uncertainty-related stress - can help us navigate stormy weather, there are other things we can do to maintain our calm and focus during these periods. Here a few simple tips to hold on to. Keep these in mind in times when you feel overwhelmed with uncontrollable events or when having to deal with unknown circumstances.

Exercise

Physical activities are an excellent outlet in so many circumstances. Whether you feel wound-up or completely lethargic, intensive exercise can help stabilize your mood and clear your mind. Among many of its benefits, exercise increases blood flow, reduces cortisol (stress hormone) levels, increases the production of endorphins, and creates a sense of lightness and wellbeing. An intensive exercise session can help you tap back into your breathing and regulate your emotions. If you enjoy team sports all the best, this will provide a chance to connect with others and enjoy camaraderie while getting all the benefits of a workout.

Not feeling particularly athletic or in the mood for strenuous exertion? No worries. At whichever pace you choose, a long walk can be very soothing and can also be a moment to ground yourself through mindfulness.

Speak up

Surrounding ourselves with people who have a positive mindset is an excellent way to tap into it ourselves. Your tribe is everything. Think about one or more people you can turn to in times of need. These people cannot be those around you who are constantly inundated in drama or persistently negative. You might select family members, close friends, colleagues, or someone else you feel comfortable being yourself around, someone in which you can happily and easily confide.

Meditate

Taking a moment to pause and observe your thoughts can only be beneficial beyond expectations. Allocate some time every day to tap out of the hustle and bustle, and sit with yourself in a quiet spot. Introspection and thought observation are highly beneficial in gaining perspective. This will help view uncertainty from a different point of view, perhaps offering a soothing reassurance that all will come to pass, no matter how much of a struggle you put up. Furthermore, it provides a special moment to practice gratitude. Mediation is a wonderful opportunity to look back on your day and bring to light everything that you are grateful for, from the roof over your head to the caring people in your life.

DIVERSIONS

Unless used for avoidance, a diversion can be calming and help steer the focus away from the constant stress of uncertainty. Diversions include anything that entertains you, usually a hobby or pastime. Don't have a hobby? Find one! Reading, painting, gardening, watching movies, playing a musical instrument, dancing...the options are endless. Having something pleasant to turn to in times of stress can be life-changing.

SORT yourself out

Although an excessive amount of this can impede you from moving forward, a balanced approach can be relaxing and offer a sense of control. I am talking about tidying. Yes, cleaning and sorting and organizing; clearing, scrubbing, washing. Although some people will retch at the idea of doing this for fun, it can procure a short-term sense of accomplishment and control over one's environment. Cleaning can be therapeutic, although it is handy to be aware that it can turn into an obsession. If this is your chosen coping method, perhaps you should add a hint of moderation to that cleaning solution.

. . .

STOP SWIMMING **against the current**

Living with uncertainty can elicit existential crises in the manner of hopelessness, despair, and depression because of the feeling that your contributions amount to nothing. Many people struggle with this, a sense of powerlessness based on the future's unpredictable challenges. This is why we seek to control, avoid confrontation, and surrender to some situations.

There are countless things that we cannot control or change, but one thing we can do is choose how we respond. You can decide to be your own most dependable and reliable person. You can choose to show up for yourself every single time.

Accepting the reality of uncertainty and being able to better manage it requires a change in perspective. The place to begin is to understand that yielding to the forces of life rather than opposing them can be a tremendous relief. Once you fully acknowledge that uncertainty is beyond your control, you can let yourself flow and experience life fully. It will most likely be uncomfortable at first, but surrendering to the natural order of things is a far easier and more beneficial option than fighting against them.

Sometimes we try to control our uncertainties through worrying and feeling anxious, fearful, or impatient. We may start overthinking things, which is highly inadvisable. Although it may seem like we are preparing for all possible outcomes within the circumstances, overthinking merely deepens the gap between being calm and collected, and ultimately losing control over our thoughts and emotional reactions. It confuses us and leads us to become embroiled in our fears and anxieties instead of logically reacting to them. A sufficient amount of stress can also activate our fight or flight response, through which our nervous system may mislead us into falsely interpreting a situation. What was initially a position of discomfort has now escalated into a full-blown emotional meltdown.

When we view a situation from a negative viewpoint and conclude that it will defeat us, we then operate from a position of fear. This is a sneaky way our body responds as it short circuits our brain, making us unable to regulate emotions and direct our focus. You can practice being open and accepting of challenges by reprogramming your thoughts. Using positive statements is an effective technique. Positive affirmations tend to lead to positive outcomes, or at least, they will look more positive from your viewpoint. Remember, most of what happens to us is reliant on perceptions. One same situation can be viewed differently by several people. Therefore, if you can't change the situation, why not alter your perception?

THE TRUTH IS, by fighting your reality and attempting to change things beyond your control, you are only making things worse. Now, giving up fighting does not mean giving up trying to make your life better in ways that you see fit! It simply means you need to reconnect with yourself and learn how to greet challenges differently. There is no need to complain; things are what they are. Life will always present a number of things that are out of your control, and that is absolutely fine because you can learn to cope healthily with anything that comes your way.

JUST FLOW

Adopting a flexible standpoint instead of being rigid has been proven, time and again, to be the best and healthiest response to challenges. We need to come to terms with the fact that life itself isn't perfect and find peace with anything that is put in our path. We can study situations and learn our own lessons from them. Make peace with the fact that no matter your level of certainty about something, nothing is set in stone. If your initial reaction is disappointment, it is up to decide if you wish to live with this feeling or let it go. Let's work towards being content with not knowing everything. True happiness comes from our capacity to embrace the unknown, to enjoy and respect it, and learn to flow.

 "Uncertainty is the only certainty there is, and knowing how to live with insecurity is the only security."

— JOHN ALLEN PAULOS

THERE IS a mental state concept called *flow,* which was coined by Hungarian-American author and psychologist Mihaly Csikszentmihalyi. In his search to determine what makes a life worth living following traumatic events and the loss of everything you hold dearly, Csikszentmihalyi began to investigate different patterns that might determine happiness. In doing so, he discovered that many people felt an incomparable sense of fulfillment when they were in this altered state of mind, a state that made them feel at one with what they were doing. The psychologist recalls interviewing a music composer who would get lost in a state of complete oneness with his music when composing. Flow is a situation where time ceases to exist, described by Csikszentmihalyi as "the state of total immersion while doing an activity." In his recent work, he also indicates that "flow comes from the intense concentration around your own actions and their immediate feedback." (Csikszentmihalyi, 2008)

KEEPING THIS IN MIND, perhaps we can try to recall when in our lives we have been in that state. Flow usually occurs when we are doing something engaging, something we are passionate about, and of which we are fluent and knowledge-able. When, in everyday life, do we actually feel happy, excited, inspired? Csikszentmihalyi revealed that many reaped the benefits of happiness not by doing things that brought them fame or fortune, but by being engaged in something they loved, during which they felt like the world has stopped.

It has been suggested that real happiness and content-ment come from being so involved in a process that we lose sight of other things; it is a mental state of complete and energized focus. We are so immersed in what we are doing that we become unaware of other distracting factors.

We spend so much time worrying about things that have barely anything to do with us, as well as situations that we have no control over. What we must do is follow the advice of Steve Marabol, who advises: "You must learn to let go. Release the stress. You were never in control anyway." He is telling us to stop trying to keep a firm hold on people, things, and events. It is a losing battle, one that will exhaust and stress you beyond measure. In time, this takes a horrible toll on our minds and bodies.

. . .

THIS LEADS us to our next point: when our reactions to uncertainty are not adaptive, we cannot expect to flow with the current. Opting for an adaptive approach allows us to just go with it; to adjust how we respond in a smooth, centered, and balanced manner. This does not imply being entirely passive, but simply to let go of what you cannot control. Flow teaches us that whatever happens, no matter our lives' circumstances, we can always tap into this inner power. Flow is pure passion, pure being, absolute presence in the moment.

Be ready to engage with your issues. Sit with your uncertainty and let it pass through.

Imagine yourself floating like a starfish in pristine turquoise waters. As your body moves to the rhythm of the swell, you float upwards and down, unknowing of what the next wave will bring. Perhaps it will submerge you and take you under, only for a moment, or maybe longer. Maybe it will raise you higher and higher, anticipation and excitement filling your soul.

Such is the way of life; a series of motions, riding the waves of the unknown, hoping for the best while accepting the extent of possibilities. Everything comes to pass, so it is up to you to choose how you want to go through the storm. You could choose to focus on the possible negative outcomes of any situation or decide to try your best with what you actually know, using the tools at hand. You could focus on what might be and what might have been, but wouldn't it be more productive to concentrate your energy on what is here in the now? Through involvement and engagement, we learn the lessons that life has in store for us; no growth can come from avoidance. Be at peace with the unknown; welcome it, respect it, and enjoy it. Let things flow. Create a unique experience for yourself and live your life to the fullest.

. . .

THE POWER of Resilience

No matter its evolution level, the human brain is designed to protect you, and it does this by underestimating the positive while overestimating the negative. We are often drawn to negativity because it provokes a reaction within us. Negative news such as job loss, death, and economic collapse puts our brains on high alert and allows us to prepare for negative outcomes.

Although this is how we naturally view and respond to life's challenges, fighting and avoiding are not advisable ways to approach adversity.

Resilience is the ability to bounce back. It is your ability to get back up after a fall and rise stronger as you move towards your future. Only by facing adversity and surrounding ourselves with love can we build resilience. Furthermore, I will repeat this; it is crucial to face our traumas and deal with emotions if we want to move forward, into a comfortable place within ourselves. In fact, resilience expert Boris Cyrulnik mentions, "Triggering a process of resilience is about escaping the prison of our past." (Cyrulnik, 2020) Greeting each day as a clean slate, without dwelling on past mistakes or misfortunes, is an essential factor for healing and mental wellbeing.

OUR BELIEFS AFFECT what we see and the way we interpret situations. Outcomes are not always within our control. We can battle through life to keep controlling everything that happens to us, or we can experience life fully, floating through, making decisions to the best of our knowledge, and have our own backs when things go sour. Extend the favors and appreciation you would offer a good friend to yourself. Why not? Why not be our own hero, our own best friend? There is no shame in feeling whole. As a matter of fact, it makes it easier to admit our mistakes, forgive our past, and move forward. It makes it easier to build resilience. It makes for more authentic relationships and a complete sense of self.

This is the basis of resilience. It is the capacity to respond to the challenges of life by being flexible and adaptive. Go ahead, let yourself float mindfully through the motions. Accept things as they are, through a state of equanimity.

Our set of unconscious and conscious beliefs create this type of mindset. This can determine how you respond in moments of uncertainty, how you perceive yourself, and how you relate to others. This mindset is a totality of who you are and how you tell your story.

You will be able to perceive things more clearly because of your ability to float mindfully through the motions of life, in such a manner that you are not focused on what is going on around you but rather on that which is going on inside you. It leaves room for perspective and allows for a unique connection into yourself, as it is a way to see further than what your eyes are telling you.

So many important lessons can be taken away from unfortunate circumstances. If you can see past your misfortunes, you may find an abundance of lessons in disguise. Seek opportunities to learn about yourself, about your strengths and weaknesses, and how you react to distressing situations. Being able to embrace your challenges mindfully and learn from them will pave the way for wisdom.

Such is the way of life; a series of motions, riding the waves of the unknown, hoping for the best while accepting the extent of possibilities. Uncertainty is unavoidable. To make the most of our short time here, we must turn to acceptance rather than resistance. Adjusting to the motions and being adaptive is crucial to gaining perspective. Everything comes to pass, so it is up to you to choose how you want to go through the storm.

6

GROWING PAINS

"Out of your vulnerabilities will come your strength."

— SIGMUND FREUD

ONE OF THE characteristics of a living being is growth. Whether it is physical, emotional, mental, or social, this characteristic is ever-present. As we all scramble to figure out our lives and provide a sense to our existence, we undoubtedly experience ups and downs. Some of us rise very high and crash very low. Others keep a steady, uneventful pace – which is not necessarily a bad thing. As you move forward and create your path, you are building yourself – up or down – as you remove some bits and adjust others. Sometimes we see ourselves having to remove big chunks of "us," such as relationships that may no longer serve us. Sometimes we replace pieces, take out the old unproductive or pointless parts, upgrade to a new way of being, or perhaps adopt a new perspective. Now, we all want to be able to move from where we are to another point as fast as we can. Wouldn't it be nice to get there sooner, to skip through the discomfort and pain of break-ups, dieting, adopting a new exercise regimen, and confronting family members? The truth is that it cannot be done by the snap of a finger. Shortcuts rarely provide the same outcome and benefits as taking the long road. Doing the work builds strength. You cannot gain strength without building resistance. That's not how things work, physically and mentally. We must go through the process of traveling the distance between these two points. We must attempt to make it past the ups and downs in order to come out stronger, through failures and successes.

So, how can we go about this inward growth process? In the first place, it is about adopting an open-minded attitude. This allows for new ideas to be noticed and considered. It leaves space for the 'new' to come in, and as it tries to make its way into your life, you will notice the old patterns, relationships, and thoughts that are no longer of service. These will be discarded to create new space, and you will be able to greet opportunities openly. Remaining open-minded and keeping a positive focus on things that matter can alter your entire approach to life. It will shift you from a 'can't do' perspective to a 'can do' mindset.

GETTING RID of unproductive and limiting thought patterns, such as chronic negativity or constant apprehension, will ultimately steer you towards opportunities and positivity.

Strive to become yourself and conquer any obstacle that will prevent that from happening. Let go of what you can't control, stop complaining, and dwelling on your past. Dismiss procrastination – it is the ultimate trap! Face life head-on; each day is for you to seize.

Now, growing out of our old ways and shedding our spurious identities is not an easy feat. This growth process is not only challenging but also painful. Shedding off these limiting parts of us may imply facing certain truths that we have been avoiding. It may mean sacrificing relationships that no longer serve us, and it may lead us to question everything we've held for certain since our youth. There's a pain that greets the action of peeling off a part of us that we have known for years to reveal who we are underneath the lies, self-doubts, and untruths. It is comparable to trying to break free from the hold of addiction.

But only through shedding its skin can a caterpillar eventually become a butterfly.

OBSTACLES TO LIVING **your truth**

Humans are anatomically, biochemically, and physiologically the same, but even with this similarity in morphology, we are all very different individuals.

So many factors influence who we are and who we eventually become. Everyone has a unique life path. Our differences are what make us exactly who we are; they characterize our individuality. Yet, we are much too often willing to dismiss our authenticity to gain external approval and please others. Indeed there's another way to feel accepted and live our truth.

The fact is, we can only feel like our own true selves when we fully express these differences and live in full truthfulness and openness. Living your truth implies fully embracing yourself as a person. No matter what you do, there will always be judgment. Can you shine your uniqueness past the comments and criticism of your peers?

Remember to beware of perfectionism. It is a trap and is merely the result of incessant self-doubt. You are not here to reach for and fulfill the potential of others. Live by your rules, by that which you believe in and put into practice. Abide by your personal values, the ones you've established, the ones that you nurture and set forth in every aspect of your life. It is crucial that you live your truth as it is the foundation upon which you build your life. It will influence everything - your relationships, your career, your emotions, and your wellbeing. Not living by your convictions can be likened to building a life based on a foundation of untruths, fabrications, misinterpretations, and denial.

As good as living your truth can be, many obstacles may stand in your way. All these stumbling blocks can prevent you from being your real self if you allow them to do so. A few of the obstacles that impede our ability to speak our minds may be linked to judgment, societal conventions, social pressure, family values and expectations, and mental health stigmas. However, when it comes to your boundaries, you always have the final verdict. Complying with others' demands and wishes is not the only option for living peacefully and feeling accepted. There are ways to experiment and grow into this. Opting for self-affirmation rather than people-pleasing is daunting at first and tends to stir up insecurities, which can make us feel worse than we initially felt. But if approached in a scaled, mindful manner, self-affirmation can lead to more respectful relationships and a well-rounded sense of belonging.

Every opinion and judgment that is not serving you,

whether they are external or internal judgment, must be removed. Judgment has the capacity to let you doubt yourself and so prevent your true potential from bursting out.

Speak your mind! You are unique, and so you should express your truth. Not only is this an essential aspect of your personal development, but it is also incredibly valuable to others. The more you stand your ground and speak your mind, the more others around you will feel comfortable following in your steps. Within respectful parameters, expressing different opinions and ideas can lead to more openness, acceptance, non-judgment, the betterment of self, and innovation.

It would be a fallacy to claim that we are all born the same; on some level, we are, but it is clear that socioeconomic status is a strong indicator of which road we will follow in life. Unfortunately, social conventions, capitalism, and the media's influence are powerful components of our world. All of these affect our emotional wellbeing and act as guidelines to our belief systems. This makes us believe we should act, look, and live a certain way.

On the other hand, you don't have to claim authority, be very wealthy, or have political or social influence to be your true self. An over-inflated ego and the ability to use it to one's advantage does not exonerate someone from possessing all primary human attributes. On some foundational level, we are all equal. Your value is yours to create.

The idea is not for you to design a new system of living your life. It is intended to rid yourself of the need to fit into a mold designed to keep us within a particular frame. If following the crowd implies sacrificing your ethics and morals, perhaps it is not as beneficial to your wellbeing as you may have believed. In time, you can learn to distinguish that which will be in your best interest and discard all that isn't beneficial.

THE POWER of NO

There are deeply ingrained patterns of needing to please others that are sabotaging our sense of self. When we grow up with this "need to please" mindset, it is difficult to break out of the pattern. The belief that what makes us good enough to be loved or respected by others is their ability to comply with their demands and wishes. We can easily get lost between what is true, what is right, and the authentic expression of our thoughts. Contenting others should not come at a personal cost.

Continuously relying on external validation has its price to pay; it is the ultimate sacrifice of your true self. Think about it: unable to internally validate yourself, you turn to others to order or confirm your thoughts, words, and actions. Where are *you* underneath all of this? There can be no sense of self-value or self-respect without a full understanding of self, governed by internal validation. Only you can know your truth, only you can own it, and only you can speak it. No one else has walked in your shoes, nor will they ever. In case you are still in doubt, this is a gentle reminder that people speak in accordance with their own baggage, issues, and self-concept. You can never offend someone unless they *choose* to take offense. Outside perspectives usually have nothing to do with you, as people tend to think of others as representations of themselves. Some advice and outside perspectives might be helpful, but ultimately it is up to you to decide what meets your needs and how to get there.

. . .

THE CHILDHOOD SCRIPT of living your life just to gratify others' needs to be discarded and rewritten. You can no longer afford to live your life like this. Learning to say NO, loud and clear, is a beautiful gift you must offer yourself. Refusing to make choices based on what people want and expect of you will change your life. Will it be challenging? Sure. Actually, it will most definitely be testing at first. But just like any habit, as you develop your strength of character and self-assuredness, you will witness how people adapt to the standards you've set. And what about those who can't stand the heat? They usually end up leaving the kitchen. Just think of how empowering and rewarding it will be to claim yourself back. Like every step in this growth process, it will take courage, determination, and resilience. Throughout this process, you will find peace of mind and a sense of wellbeing as you claim control over your life, your choices, and their outcomes.

When we ceaselessly attempt to please others, we deprive ourselves of keeping hold of valuable pieces of our authentic being. Being overly agreeable can come at a dear price. It is often a sacrifice of self-respect, integrity, self-esteem, and identity. It generates negative feelings towards oneself, constantly criticizing and belittling what we think and do. Shame, one of the most damaging emotional states, is also a derivation of being unable to set boundaries. Brené Brown says it best: "I define shame as the intensely painful feeling or experience of believing that we are flawed and therefore unworthy of love and belonging – something we've experienced, done, or failed to do makes us unworthy of connection." (Brown, 2013) Persistently viewing yourself as lesser than others and not good enough is harmful to the mind and the body. What's more, chronic insecurity leaves you at the mercy of others' better judgment – which is not a safe and happy place to be.

THIS HAS BEEN one of the biggest battles of my life, and I am no longer ashamed to say that it is an ongoing recovery process. We are not programmed to stand tall to be strong and to take pride. Somehow along the way, humility has become a synonym for belittling ourselves so as not to offend others' pride. I now understand and remind myself constantly that the contentment of others cannot be detrimental to my wellbeing. Why should I respect others and not my own person? In that aspect, we must put ourselves first. I encourage you to use the tools offered here (reflection, mediation, talk therapy) to find comfort in self-validation. Understand that you are enough; that you are worthy of love, respect, and dignity, just as is anyone else.

Learning to say NO is pure art. The workings around self-affirmation are complex. For some of us, it comes easily; for others, it is the battle of a lifetime. In situations of doubt as to whether you are being true to yourself or merely being agreeable, you can opt to remove yourself and think about what you want and what feels right. And if this creates an adverse reaction from the other party involved, I would like to remind you that it does not matter. Others are entitled to express their emotions, and this is never a reflection on you. I like to think that we don't owe anything but respect. Refusing to make life choices based on what people want from you is the most important, reflecting respect for oneself.

RECOGNIZING toxicity

The term "toxic" is often used to describe substances capable of causing severe harm and debilitation. In our quest to reconnect with our true selves, we must learn to recognize toxicity in our environment. Toxicity can be found in many forms, including destructive relationships, an unhealthy work environment, and self-damaging habits. It can often be attributed to negative places, behaviors, thoughts, and individuals.

Once you've established your fundamental principles and boundaries, these toxic patterns in your life tend to become more evident. This is not surprising, as, at this point, you will feel more in control of your needs and wants, making it possible to see clearly that which does not serve you.

When these unwanted aspects of your life begin to appear, you will be confronted with difficult choices. It can be challenging and daunting to accept that some habits and people are no longer beneficial to your wellbeing. It may feel like a revelation, but deep down, we all know that our intuitive self was light years ahead of our consciousness. At this stage, you will undoubtedly need to take some time to pause and reflect. You may find it useful to whip out a piece of paper and jot down the positive versus negative for every element you doubt. In doing this, remember that not all confronting aspects need to be immediately discarded. It is up to you to reach inwards into your intuitive self, as well as into your rational self, to determine what will bring you emotional balance.

Some indicators can help us pinpoint what is not of service to us. Feeling worse after an interaction can sometimes be an indicator of toxicity. Whatever it is that manipulates you, takes advantage of you for their own benefit, makes you feel less of yourself, and causes abuse or harm to you in any way can be said to bring toxicity into your life.

. . .

As a general guideline, elements that bring out the worst in you should be eliminated from your life. For example, if one of your personal values is to act and speak positively whenever possible, you may want to stay away from people who cultivate and thrive on negativity. There is much truth in the proverb "misery likes company." We attract what we encompass and project to the world. Furthermore, it is part of human nature to seek that which is familiar or alike. Knowing this, the power is in your hands to create an environment you can thrive in and to reach your full potential in accordance with your values.

Now, understand that being toxic may sometimes not mean that people or environments are fundamentally wrong, but simply that they are harmful to you. Those unhealthy patterns may only appear when you interact with them... and that's ok! We are all different and have distinct needs. These elements don't have to be labeled as "bad," but instead dismissed as not being of service to you. With this neutral mindset, it becomes easy to release toxicity without feeling guilt, sadness, or frustration.

Shifting your perceptions

The mind can be likened to a stream. Just like the water that flows through, your thoughts waver in and out. Just as a stream flows without anyone's input or control, thoughts also tend to drift in and out of your mind without being pushed to do so. They come from everywhere and nowhere. They can leave a deep imprint or vanish like dust.

Every second of each day, this stream flows steadily.

You don't create your thoughts, but you do experience

them. In that sense, you have no power to select most of what may pop into your mind, but you do possess the ability to choose how you react to your thoughts. There are many strategies linked to the practice of mindfulness and meditation that facilitate the regulation of emotional responses. Being aware of our thoughts and consciously holding on to or dismissing them takes practice.

When you are operating from a position of unawareness, you can't observe your thoughts and realize which ones to hold on to. You are only reacting to things that pop into your head. As a result, you become swept away by them, as well as by the emotional response they resuscitate.

Identifying your thoughts is an essential first step in regulating your response. When you pay attention to a specific idea, perhaps one that is bothering you, you are already acknowledging its existence. This then enables you to make a conscious decision as to whether you will allow it to permeate your emotions or let it float on and back to where it came from. If you were to speak to that thought, it would sound something like this: "I know you are there, but you are not real. You are not needed. Please move along and away." The same goes for thoughts that serve your purpose; you might decide to hold on to those that will benefit you. The point is, you are not a victim of your thoughts, but rather the ultimate decider. Cultivating such a frame of mind will help you develop awareness and shift perceptions, making it possible to push aside judgment and preconceived ideas.

THE COMPARISON TRAP

 "Comparison is the thief of joy."

— Theodore Roosevelt

∼

Our differences are what make us strong and allow us to distinguish ourselves from the crowd. Comparing ourselves to others in order to measure how well we are moving along through life is a habit we develop from an early age. We've all been condition to follow certain societal parameters, this intangible guideline labeled normality. What, in fact, does it mean to be "normal"? What is usually attributed to the spectrum of normality refers to that which is average, that of which most people adhere to. Normality is highly subjective and varies in different societal frames. Normality also implies conformity, and as we've previously explored, conformity is one way in which we lose our sense of self.

When you compare yourself to other people, whether based on job performance, wealth, looks, social abilities, or even social media popularity, you are disempowering yourself. It is impossible to stand your ground and live authentically while you are comparing yourself to others. To live a full life in a complete self-expanded state, the only fruitful comparison you should make is to your old self.

Focusing on others' achievements or successes can be beneficial if it inspires us to move forward. However, comparisons tend to reflect that which we yearn for, or wish to be, which leads to victimizing ourselves. We unknowingly place ourselves in a "lesser" category, creating those limiting thought patterns. This is a fast track to chronic dissatisfaction and unhappiness. All it ever does is keep us focused on what we hate about ourselves and our lives. It steals away valuable energy, time, and effort that would have been better expended on building a better tomorrow. If only that energy could be shifted into observing our own potential and working towards bettering ourselves in accordance with our goals and principles, we could become unstoppable. It is surprising how often the most significant obstacles to living a fulfilling life are within our self.

You have to take back your power, which you have given away to people, situations, and places. To move past this incessant comparing, you must make a clear and conscious choice to clean up your self-deprecating thoughts. Because that is, in fact, precisely what you are submitting yourself to when you belittle yourself in such a way. Others are free to succeed or fail; the way they live their lives has no connection to your potential to change yours. Decide not to waste your time and energy on others, but rather use it to build yourself up. Drive your focus towards being the best possible version of yourself.

When in doubt, recall all the obstacles you have already overcome. Remember your victories and celebrate how much you have progressed on your personal voyage. Life is a journey, not a race. Enjoy each step, as there are valuable teachings at every stage. Start every new day with a clean slate. You have the power to alter the future, beginning with a fresh start every minute, every single day. Whenever you are confronted with a dilemma, see it as a gift. Making choices is creating opportunities.

This is a valuable habit to put into practice. Comparing yourself to others should no longer serve you. Find that space within yourself where you can cultivate appreciation, kindness, and gratitude for what you have accomplished.

COLLATERAL DAMAGE

No other aptitude is worthier than that of truly knowing yourself. Being your authentic self means owning your own reality. It implies unapologetically acknowledging, accepting, and loving your imperfections. It is choosing to speak and live your truth and being whole and happy about it instead of living for the acceptance and gratification of others. As a natural consequence of growing into your true self, your energy will shift, and you will realize that some people and things no longer serve your purpose and so should no longer be a part of your life.

Until you are your real and authentic self, you cannot live your best life. Confidence and total fulfillment come from truly knowing yourself. Make decisions that improve and better your life, rather than endlessly tending to the desires of others. Find what you want, and cultivate the courage to go and get it.

One thing you must know is that the road to becoming this person isn't paved with gold. Knowing where you stand and refusing to cross boundaries is not an easy route to follow. Arriving at the point where you are nothing but your true self will demand some sacrifices and challenge your character's strength in many ways. Be prepared to have to step out of your comfort zone. It will be a crucial step in becoming the person you really are, deep down. And don't think that this will always be a challenge; as the saying goes, *practice makes perfect*. As you put into place that which you choose to adhere to and act in full support of your values and principles, you will notice an evolution take place. You will see that some things that previously felt daunting have become a natural habit.

On your journey, there will be many things of which to let go and many other new ones to embrace. Mistakes will be made, have no doubt! But you will develop the strength to greet these mistakes with compassion and view them as learning opportunities.

On a final note, remember that you always have the choice to hold on to something or to let go. As you grow into your new soul skin, you will begin to perceive things differently, causing you to be driven to shed what does not serve the real YOU.

Although the freedom to be your true self is fulfilling, the work one must do to achieve that state of liberty can feel terrifying. Hold on to your conviction that the challenges it brings are absolutely and completely worth it. Keep your goals and aspirations at the forefront of your mind. And please, remember that you are worth it.

7

BODY & MIND

"To keep the body in good health is a duty...
otherwise we shall not be able to keep our
mind strong and clear."

— BUDDHA

THE RELATIONSHIP between the mind and the body is not a
recent discovery. Until the 17th century, the mind and the
body were treated as one unique and indivisible whole.
Although the Western world's ideas about the lack of
connection between the body and the mind led to significant medical advances, it experienced stunted growth in
areas of emotional, psychological, and spiritual development. The healing of the physical body was connected to
extrinsic factors, such as surgery and medication. This attitude towards medicine and treatment continued until the

20th century. As things began to change, research work surfaced in the area of connections between the mind and the body. The research showed a complex but essential link between these two parts of our making. Out of this emerged a new discourse, proclaiming the benefits of mind-body practices.

I cannot tell you how many times I have been a victim of a mind-body-associated breakdown. As a child, I would spend countless hours at day-care lying on the floor in a quiet corner, attempting to cope with an endless stream of headaches and migraines. I was taken to numerous doctors, had scans and tests performed; yet, no physical ailment was ever found to be a trigger. As a teenager, I struggled with much anxiety, and these cyclical migraines persisted in making an appearance. Headaches were a daily occurrence.

Years passed, and I struggled with stress and anxiety, headaches becoming a central part of my daily life. Towards my later teen years, I joined an organized sports team, which led to me being much more active. This also created a sense of belonging within a new group of friends. High doses of strenuous physical activity combined with positive social interaction turned out to be most helpful in attenuating my headaches' frequency and strength. Much of my angst had come from not having a sense of purpose and belonging, which was appeased by this passion I had discovered.

Now, I only came to this realization many years later as an adult. I was going through a period of several life-changes that had me feeling powerless, confused as to where I belonged, and anxious. This left me in a very vulnerable state, and migraines had me feeling helpless; I could not control them, and I did not know how to prevent them. Deciding I could not live my life this way, I began to change my diet and returned to daily high-intensity exercise. I set about making plans to continue traveling abroad, which had always been one of my heart's deepest desires.

When I finally set out to do things my way, follow my dreams, and lead with my heart, I unleashed a dormant potential. I realized that when my mind was strong and fulfilled, my body responded in much the same way. My headaches still appeared at times, but I recognized them as a friend tapping me on the shoulder, saying, "maybe you should reconsider what you're doing." And the truth is, sometimes I didn't listen and pushed forward anyway, avoiding my intuition and following my rational thoughts. And every single time, a migraine ensued.

If there is any advice I can offer from what I have learned, it is that our minds and bodies are connected in such a privileged way that it would be shameful to dismiss the signals we receive. Our physical body and psyche are interlinked and are continuously communicating messages to us, responding to our environment in view of where we stand. Although my life's challenges have revolved around releasing anxiety patterns, everyone has their own particular battles to fight. Remember that it is a battle in which your greatest ally lies within you; you may as well acknowledge its presence and make the most of it.

THE LINK between physical and psychological wellbeing

The complex interrelationship between the body and the mind means that your feelings, thoughts, attitudes, and beliefs have a direct relationship with the way your body works. In fact, we could almost say that our bodies respond to our psyche. Your mind impacts your body, whether negatively or positively.

Understanding this link does not permit us to heal all our

physical wounds instantly. It does, however, provide us with an opportunity to investigate the benefits of holistic healing. It can help us gain insight into our general health and offer us an alternative to modern medicinal practices. Many mind-body practices have no negative repercussions whatso-ever and can help cultivate a balanced lifestyle. Body-mind practices such as meditation, mindfulness, massage therapy, and yoga can be founded on the interrelationship between these two parts of the body. The mind affects the body, and the body affects the mind. Knowledge of alternative and preventive healing methods is empowering. Understanding the intricate workings of our body and mind allows us to make better informed health-oriented decisions. This also shifts the responsibility of our holistic wellbeing from medical practitioners back into our own hands.

Optimal wellbeing promotes the synchronistic work between the physical (body) and the psychological (mind). There exists a complex relationship between physical and mental wellbeing, as the physical part of the body is inter-connected to the psychological part.

The World Health Organization's constitution happens to indicate that "Health is a state of complete physical, mental and social wellbeing and not merely the absence of disease or infirmity. There is no health without mental health." (WHO, 1946) In that sense, veritable wellbeing consists of seamless interconnectivity between these aspects, a state of dynamic balance to create complete harmony within our being – which is all the more reason to implement holistic approaches when it comes to promoting our health and preventing diseases.

In trying to understand this mind-body connection, let's start by making some clarifications. The first thing is this: the mind isn't the same thing as the brain. Although they are intricately connected, the mind consists of mental states such as thoughts, emotions, beliefs, memories, attitudes, and desires. The mind is nonphysical, whereas the brain itself acts more like the hardware that makes it possible for these mental states to be experienced. Since these experiences are located in the body (not just in the brain), we can say the mind is in the body.

The hormones coursing through the body shape provoke and result from thoughts and emotions. For instance, testosterone brings out our competitive and self-focused side, yet it is also released when needed to reach these same outcomes. Adrenaline can make us energized or anxious, as well as being one of our stress-response protection mechanisms. Endorphins can be released with intense exercise, offering an overwhelming sense of lightness and wellbeing. Interestingly, we also possess neurotransmitters in our gut that help us respond and remember experiences, providing the physiological foundation of gut feelings and intuition.

Our immune system is, in some way, an extension of the mind by how it influences our mood and responds to psychological stress. The mind and body are connected in a constant flow of inputs and outputs. At once, they experience the cause and the consequence of our thoughts and bodily responses. What this tells us is that a healthy and happy life results from a balanced relationship between physical and psychological states. One example of this is how people who exercise regularly sleep better, are more alert and enjoy a greater sense of wellbeing. The body and mind are interconnected, and both perform significant roles in determining how we think, how we act, and the way in which we experience life.

· · ·

Gut-brain connection

Our digestive system, commonly referred to as our gut, is a central part of our physical composition. Your digestive system is responsible for vital bodily responses. Having a major influence on the development and reactions of our immune system, our gut has many functions. It is most commonly known for facilitating digestion and absorbing nutrients but does so much more. Lined with over 100 trillion bacteria and 100 million neurons, your gut is home to over 70% of your body's immunity cells. It produces a substantial number of neurotransmitters that directly connect your gut to your mind. Furthermore, over 95% of your body's serotonin, a chemical that regulates mood, is located in your gut. Often underestimated, your gut holds a predominant role in your overall mental and physical health.

What you feed your body and your mind will directly impact every aspect of your life. When your body is in good shape, you are more likely to feel in control, mentally strong, and alert. Whatever is detrimental to your mental health will often negatively impact your body and vice versa. An unwell mind can manifest its discomfort through the physical body: muscle pain, headaches, back pain, stomach ulcers, and neck stiffness – the list goes on. By understanding the link that exists between our physical and psychological wellbeing, we can opt for lifestyle choices that allow us to better manage our mental and physical health.

8

LIVING AUTHENTICALLY

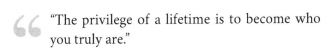

"The privilege of a lifetime is to become who you truly are."

— CARL JUNG

IN A WORLD DRIVEN BY SCREEN-OBSESSION, networking, capitalism, status, ego, and materialism, talking about authenticity can feel like a foreign concept.

Many people have so buried themselves in following the crowd that they have no idea what being themselves actually means. We are majorly followers, forced to comply to certain measures to become a functioning member of modern society. In doing so, it has been easy to dismiss our exact needs and to set aside our inner-truth.

Living authentically is about approaching life from a different perspective; it is about living life from the inside out. A life of genuine authenticity is one where our feelings, thoughts, and actions are in harmony. It is living through a state of congruency, aligning our words and actions with our beliefs and principles.

Living authentically is about being ourselves, and that must come from a place of knowing ourselves. This implies identifying your true values and beliefs and then directing your actions and words to align with them. When you're living authentically, you enjoy an inner sense of peace, contentment, and meaning. If your words and actions are not aligned with your principles and beliefs, you will come to experience internal distress. When you are in this state of cognitive dissonance, your only options to deal with this sense of unpleasantness are to change your behavior or alter your thought patterns. Your peace can be restored when your external and internal worlds align. This self-knowledge requires self-awareness, self-acceptance, and mindfulness, all of which can be developed at any stage of life.

Personal values and beliefs are not what you should be or what you should do. They come from a place of knowing deep within and are a reflection of what you hold dear. Authenticity is having values that truly represent you at your best, the genuine person you want to be, and the most veritable version of yourself. It is having beliefs that reflect how you want to go about your life, rather than what you are told you should be. The truth is, authenticity leaves no space for external compliance.

 "Happiness depends upon ourselves."

— ARISTOTLE

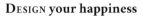

DESIGN your happiness

One of Western society's most prevalent aspects is a culture of entitlement. This is a belief that external factors are somehow responsible for our happiness, as well as the outcomes of our life. There is a tendency to transfer responsibilities to greater entities, such as blaming laws, education, financial crises, and political decisions for our lack of self-fulfillment. It is relatively easy to push the blame onto external factors, thus justifying our lack of action to direct our own lives.

Many of us have been brought up to outsource responsibility for our lives, to reach out to others for self-validation and life-direction. Blame for our unhappiness has been laid upon our parents, teachers, bosses, spouses, friends, colleagues, and countless other factors. It is our responsibility to create and build the fortress of our existence.

THE TRUTH IS that you are and always will be the only person who can determine the quality of your life. Even though the outcomes are not always within our control, we possess the power to choose how we'll ride the waves of life. Your reactions are 100% your responsibility, dictating how you experience anything and everything that comes your way and whether it is a failure or a success. You are responsible for your achievements, losses, quality of relationships, health, physical fitness level, feelings, financial situation, and psychological well-being. I cannot stress this enough: your life is entirely your responsibility.

As a side note, while creating and designing a life for ourselves, we must be selective of the people we invite to accompany us on our journey. The people you spend most of your time with have a powerful impact in determining who you will become. Make a habit of mixing with people who will raise you instead of dragging you down. It is your responsibility to completely disentangle yourself from anyone whose values or beliefs are not aligned with your own. Surround yourself with friends, family, and colleagues who act as a healthy support system – people who accept you exactly as you are and have your best interest at heart.

In addition, remember that "you are the average of the five people you associate with most, so do not underestimate the effects of your pessimistic, unambitious, or disorganized friends. If someone isn't making you stronger, they're making you weaker." (Ferris, 2007) Reach out to those who will enhance your castle, and be fearless in turning away the people or things that do not serve your kingdom. Do things that speak to your soul; this will inevitably attract like-minded people and opportunities aligned with your objectives. The type of people you allow in will be extremely influential in determining whether you remain connected to your authentic self.

For far too long, we have blamed circumstances – favorable or unfavorable – as the reason for the many happenings in our lives. Living authentically is about understanding that you are your own choice. It's about knowing that there is a correlation between action and reaction, seed and fruit, sowing, and reaping. It is knowing that you are not a victim of your circumstances but are, in fact, a product of your decisions. As per the wise words of Epictetus, Greek philosopher: "Circumstances do not make the man, they only reveal him to himself."

. . .

UPSIZE **your potential**

Humans are created for expression; it has been in our nature since the beginning of time. The only way the world can enjoy the brilliance of your truest self is through its expression. In trying to avoid judgment or protecting others' feelings, many get into the self-defeating habit of downplaying their spark.

Downplaying your strengths for the benefit of others, whether this might lead to acceptance or success, is a losing game. Judgment from others is absolutely unavoidable. Everyone is their own unique person and is entitled to possess different perceptions and opinions. As such, in making yourself less than who you truly are, you are denying yourself full ownership of your person. You are standing in your own way on your path to living a self-accomplished fulfilling life.

Downplaying your potential will prevent you from fully expressing or experiencing anything that comes your way. The truth is that no matter what you do, you will never be able to please everyone. So, you might as well make decisions that reflect your innermost values and be your own best ally. Acknowledging your worth is not bragging, nor is it something of which to feel ashamed. Recognize yourself as your best ally, and use your many strengths to your advantage.

BECOMING YOU

~

The biggest and most significant discovery we can ever undertake is that of who we truly are. As important as this journey is, only a few of us contemplate it, and even less take on this challenge. Some may view this as an inherently selfish thing to do, failing to understand the beauty of this selfless act. However, as we begin to embrace our authentic selves, we become capable of offering the best of our being to those who matter most to us. This all begins at the source, at the very core of ourselves. To find fulfilment and purpose, we must start by discovering who we are. Striving to build your life on a solid foundation of self-love and self-knowledge is of great importance and a most noble feat.

On a final note, I would like to remind you that your journey to authenticity is unique, just as you are. In the words of Anna Quindlen, "the thing that is really hard, and really amazing, is giving up on being perfect and beginning to work on becoming yourself." Take that leap into yourself.

That is the true beauty of existence: being different, completely unique, perfectly flawed, and a beautiful work-in-progress. Acknowledging our wholeness and being kind and compassionate towards ourselves is a beautiful place to start.

POSTSCRIPT

We'd love to hear your thoughts…
Please leave a review!

As an independent author with a small marketing budget, **reviews** are my livelihood on this platform. If you enjoyed this book, I would truly appreciate if you left your honest feedback. You can do this by clicking the link to *Growing Into You* at amazon.com.

Additionally, you can join our community here https://www.facebook.com/groups/theemeraldsociety, or contact me directly via ydgardens@emeraldsocpublishing.com.

I personally read every single review and it warms my heart to hear from my readers.

With Kindness,
Yas

ALSO BY Y.D. GARDENS

Growing Stronger

Awakening to Authenticity Collection

The Well-Being Handbook

Embracing Your Darkness

EMBRACING YOUR DARKNESS

This is the heart-to-heart you've been waiting for.

Lay all your cards on the table. Hold nothing back.

This is your moment to face yourself;

this is your time to heal and start anew.

Your Shadow incorporates all your disowned, unhealed parts that are hidden deep within the unconscious. The fragments of your being that form your Shadow stem from psychological pain and trauma, creating a tangled web of repressed emotional wounds.

The only way to heal is to uncover what lies beneath and embrace your darkness.

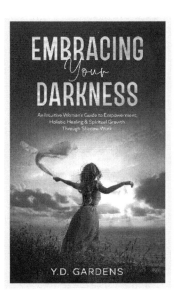

Are you ready to face your Shadow?

REFERENCES

~

Brown, B. (2017). *Braving the Wilderness: the quest for true belonging and the courage to stand alone*. Penguin Books.

Goleman, D. (1995). *Emotional Intelligence: Why it can matter more than IQ*. Bantam Books.

Brown, B. (2010). *The Gifts of Imperfection: Let go of who you think you're supposed to be and embrace who you are*. Hazelden Publishing.

Ferris, T. (2007). *The 4-Hour Work Week: Escape the 9-5, Live Anywhere and Join the New Rich*. Ebury Digital.

Brown, B. (2007). *I Thought It Was Just Me (but it isn't): Making the journey from "What Will People Think?" to "I Am Enough"*. Avery, Penguin Random House.

Kornfield, Jack. (2008). *The Art of Forgiveness, Lovingkindness and peace*. Bantam.

Brown, B. (2012). *Daring Greatly: How the Courage to be Vulnerable Transforms the Way We Live, Love, Parent, and Lead*. Penguin UK.

Mindfulness. (n.d.) *In Oxford Learner's Dictionaries*. Retrieved from https://www.oxfordlearnersdictionaries.com

Martin, S. (2020, January 24). The Need to Please: The Psychology of People-Pleasing [Blog post]. Retrieved from https://blogs.psychcentral.com/imperfect/2020/01/the-need-to-please-the-psychology-of-people-pleasing/

Taylor, J. (2012) Personal Growth: Your Values, Your Life: Are you living your life in accordance with your values? [Blog post]. Retrieved from https://www.psychologytoday.com/us/blog/the-power-prime/201205/personal-growth-your-values-your-life

Parker, T. (2016). 6 Steps to Mindfully Deal with Difficult Emotions. [Blog post]. Retrieved from https://www.gottman.com/blog/6stepstomindfullydealwithdifficultemotions/

Vilhauer, J. (2018). 3 Effective Visualization Techniques to Change Your Life. [Blog post]. Retrieved from https://www.psychologytoday.com/us/blog/living-forward/201806/3-effective-visualization-techniques-change-your-life

Strauss Cohen, I. (2017). Important Tips on How to Let Go and Free Yourself. [Blog post]. Retrieved from https://www.psychologytoday.com/us/blog/your-emotional-meter/201708/important-tips-how-let-go-and-free-yourself

Ni, P. (2013). Are You Too Nice? 7 Ways to Gain Appreciation & Respect. [Blog post]. Retrieved from https://www.psychologytoday.com/us/blog/communication-success/201309/are-you-too-nice-7-ways-gain-appreciation-respect

Streep, P. (2020). Using Visualization to Calm Yourself and Manage Your Emotions (Even Now). [Blog post]. Retrieved from https://blogs.psychcentral.com/knotted/2020/03/using-visualization-to-calm-yourself-and-manage-your-emotions-even-now/

Stanborough, R.J. (2019) What Are Cognitive Distortions

And How Can You Change These Thinking Patterns? Retrieved from https://www.healthline.com/health/cognitive-distortions#thought-origins

Strauss Cohen, I. (2018) The Search for Your True Self: Important tips on how to know our true desires. [Blog post] Retrieved from https://www.psychologytoday.com/us/blog/your-emotional-meter/201806/the-search-your-true-self

TED (2011, January 3) *The power of vulnerability | Brené Brown*. [Video] Retrieved from YouTube. URL https://www.youtube.com/watch?v=iCvmsMzlF7o

Chesak, J. (2018). The No BS Guide to Protecting Your Emotional Space. *Healthline*. Retrieved from https://www.healthline.com/health/mental-health/set-boundaries#how-to-communicate-and-set-your-boundaries

World Health Organization. (2020). *WHO Constitution*. [Webpage] Retrieved from https://www.who.int/about/who-we-are/constitution

World Health Organization. (2020). *WHO Mental Health*. [Webpage] Retrieved from https://www.who.int/health-topics/mental-health#tab=tab_1

Kendrick, T., & Pilling, S. (January 2012). Common mental health disorders - identification and pathways to care: NICE Clinical Guideline [PDF]. Retrieved from https://www.ncbi.nlm.nih.gov/pmc/articles/PMC3252532/pdf/bjgp62-047.pdf

Lussier, M. (July 2018). *The Impact Psychological Well Being Has on Physical Health*. [Blog post] Retrieved from https://www.unh.edu/healthyunh/blog/psychological-health/2018/07/impact-psychological-well-being-has-physical-health

MacMillan, A. (February 2017). Why Mental Illness Can Fuel Physical Disease. *Time* [Magazine] https://time.com/4679492/depression-anxiety-chronic-disease/

Wilks, D. *The Link Between Mental and Physical Wellbeing*.

[Article] Retrieved from https://www.myhealth1st.com.au/health-hub/articles/the-link-between-mental-health-and-physical-wellbeing/

Harvard Medical School – Healthbeat. *Good balance requires mental and physical fitness*. [Article] Retrieved from https://www.health.harvard.edu/staying-healthy/good-balance-requires-mental-and-physical-fitness

McGonigal, K. (August 2012). Is You Mind Separate From Your Body? How mind-body beliefs shape your choices and influence your health. *Psychology Today*. Retrieved from https://www.psychologytoday.com/us/blog/the-science-willpower/201208/is-your-mind-separate-your-body

Greco, V., & Roger, D. (April 2003). Personalities and Individual Differences: uncertainty, stress, and health. [Web-page] Retrieved from https://www.researchgate.net/publication/223850969_Uncertainty_stress_and_health

Raab, D. (August 2018). Deep Secrets and Inner Child Healing: research shows that being in touch with your inner child is healing. *Psychology Today*. Retrieved from https://www.psychologytoday.com/us/blog/the-empowerment-diary/201808/deep-secrets-and-inner-child-healing

Raypole, C. (June 2020). Finding and Getting to Know Your Inner Child. *Healthline*. Retrieved from https://www.healthline.com/health/inner-child

Goldminz, I. (September 2018). Emotional Reasoning and other Cognitive Distortions. [Blog post] Retrieved from https://medium.com/org-hacking/emotional-reasoning-and-other-cognitive-distortions-b01f5464d891

Lerner, H. (2004). *Fear and Other Uninvited Guests: Tackling the Anxiety, Fear and Shame that keep us from Optimal Living and Loving*. Harper.

TED (February 2004) *Flow, the secret to happiness | Mihaly Csikszentmihalyi*. [Video] Retrieved from TED: Ideas Worth

Spreading. URL https://www.ted.com/talks/ mihaly_csikszentmihalyi_flow_the_secret_to_happiness? language=en#t-630037

Spirit of Humanity Forum. *What is resilience? Interview with Dr. Boris Cyrulnik.* [Webpage] Retrieved from https:// www.sohforum.org/2020/01/22/what-is-resilience- interview-with-dr-boris-cyrulnik/

Brown, B. (January 2013). *shame v. guilt.* [Blog post] Retrieved from https://brenebrown.com/blog/2013/01/14/ shame-v-guilt/

Earl E. Bakken Center for SPIRITUALITY & HEALING. (2016) *Taking Charge of your Health & wellbeing: What is the Mind-Body Connection?* [Webpage] Retrieved from
https://www.takingcharge.csh.umn.edu/what-is-the- mind-body-connection

Danone Nutricia Research. *Gut and Microbiology: The central role of the gut.* [Webpage] Retrieved from https://www. nutriciaresearch.com/gut-and-microbiology/the-central- role-of-the-gut/

Brain Quotes: Inspire & Motivate. *Greatest Tragedies in Life Quotes* [Webpage] Retrieved from http://www. braintrainingtools.org/skills/one-of-the-greatest-tragedies- in-life-is-to-lose-your-own-sense-of-self-and-meaning/

Good Reads. *Quotable Quote: Lao Tzu, Tao Te Ching.* [Web- page] Retrieved from https://www.goodreads.com/quotes/ 2979-knowing-others-is-intelligence-knowing-yourself-is- true-wisdom-mastering

Evolve with Lou: Empowering You. *As I began to love myself... .* [Webpage] Retrieved from https://evolvewithlou. com/as-i-began-to-love-myself/

Healthline. *Finding and Getting to Know Your Inner Child.* [Webpage] Retrieved from https://www.healthline.com/ health/inner-child

Institute Success. *Eckhart Tolle*. [Webpage] Retrieved from https://institutesuccess.com/library/when-you-become-comfortable-with-uncertainty-infinite-possibilities-open-up-in-your-life-eckhart-tolle/

Good Reads. *Quotable Quotes: John Allen Paulos*. [Webpage] Retrieved from https://www.goodreads.com/quotes/504787-uncertainty-is-the-only-certainty-there-is-and-knowing-how

The Tavistok Insistute. *Sigmund Freud*. [Webpage] Retrieved from https://www.tavinstitute.org/news/out-of-your-vulnerabilities-will-come-your-strength-sigmund-freud/

Shaw, M. *Why is comparison the thief of joy and how to stop comparing yourself to others*. [Webpage] Retrieved from https://madeleineshaw.com/why-comparison-is-the-thief-of-joy-and-how-to-stop-comparing-yourself-to-others/

Pass It On. *Quotes: Ralph Waldo Emerson*. [Webpage] Retrieved from https://www.passiton.com/inspirational-quotes/3392-what-lies-behind-us-and-what-lies-before-us

Good Reads. *Quotable Quotes: Carl Gustav Jung.* [Webpage] Retrieved from https://www.goodreads.com/quotes/75948-the-privilege-of-a-lifetime-is-to-become-who-you

Brainy Quotes. *Aristotle Quotes*. [Webpage] Retrieved from https://www.brainyquote.com/quotes/aristotle_138768

Made in the USA
Middletown, DE
06 November 2023

42026960R00085